152l

Divorced Dads' Rules For Raising *Relatively* Stable Kids

By Patrick L. Talley

This book as well as other creations by
Patrick Talley is available for purchase at:
http://www.amazon.com &
http://www.createspace.com

Please visit my website and leave comments at
http://www.divorceddadsrules.com

FLASHGOODMAN PRINTING
Houston, Texas, USA

Author's Preface

I want to take a moment to thank those who put their energy into this book's creation and evolution. This book has been a lifetime in coming together – my lifetime.

To my kids, Alyssa and Connor, I say, "Thank You". You've both held up the mirror on countless occasions to allow me to see the father who I want to be, to see the man who I want to be. At times, I stepped up to the plate and took a yard. At other times, I stumbled as if I were wearing clown shoes. And I surely was. Those times when I stumbled are now the sand to make your pearl. And what you choose to do with all those lessons is your exciting adventure. I do hope I'm around long enough to enjoy watching you two parent your own children. I love you both! I'm truly thankful that you chose me to be your dad.

To my mom and dad – wow! You two raised eight kids on less than a shoestring budget. You gave and gave to that brood, and we've all turned out to be reasonably balanced adults. You buried one son and continued to raise seven more children together. That's a feat that most statisticians would say is almost unheard of. Even through it all, there was ample love and lots of hugs. At almost sixty years of marriage you are a great example of the word "commitment". It is because of you two that I now have this big ol' goofy family who puts the *funk* in dysfunctional. Some of your children, mom and dad, have chosen the parenting role and to observe them is to surely see that you have set a great example. I can't thank you enough for showing me the way.

To my friends, my boys, I say thanks for being the strong men you are and for being there to listen to my struggles as a parent. You know who you are, but I'll put your names in ink nonetheless – Bijoy, Ed, BA, Booty, Jeff, and Dan. I've learned from each of you, and my kids are the better for it.

Now this book would have not been possible, 'cause I would have blown my brains out long ago, if it weren't for my greatest of child rearing mentors, my sister Suzanne. She is our family's matriarch in the wings. She raised two of her own and took in another, and all are turning out to be good to great young adult men. Suzanne, my kiddos and I would be in the nuthouse if I hadn't had your guidance and patience. My kids may end up doing some couch-time with a shrink before it's all said and done, but surely that time will be reduced because of your guidance. You've helped me through every single parenting and life challenge, and my children are the better for it. I could never thank you enough, but suffice it to say that your patience, guidance, honesty, love, and strength will carry on to future generations. You've affected the world with your love just like the proverbial ripples in the pond.

Thank you also to my ex-wife, who's been there for my children and has done her best to co-parent with me through all these years. I know it hasn't been a cakewalk due to my stubborn nature. These kids turned out all right, in spite of our struggles and stumbles.

Special thanks to Tracy Gray for editing, without her help this book would have had many more errors and taken longer to complete.

Table of Contents

FORWARD

This book is written from a man's perspective, and that should be considered at all times. I do hope that women read the book. Not so I can make more money, as you never really make any money on these deals. Rather, it may do some good for the kids of divorce if the moms can see how the dads deal with some of this stuff. This book is for the innocents of the divorce. It is written for the children. If you, as an adult, get something out of it, then it is all the better. But that's really up to you. If one kid, somewhere, turns out to lead a more peaceful life, if even only for ten minutes, because one or both of his parents read this book, then it was worth all the time I put into writing it.

This book is unlike any you have ever read or any I've ever written. That's an easy statement as this is the first book I've ever written. It's a guy's book, from guy to guy, cutting through as much of the bullshit as I can. The reason I wrote this book is because I have found over the years that I am the expert in divorce and raising kids through divorce. Okay – so I'm no expert, but I have found myself countless times counseling dads during their pending divorces or just after their divorces are final. We need to help each other to raise great kids. Hey – it takes a village.

Additionally, I probably come across as a pretty good guy in most of these stories. Hey – consider the source. If my ex-wife were writing this book, I could surely be shown in a different light. For at times I have danced elegantly in these parenting shoes, and I have stumbled like a buffoon at other times.

It's pretty easy at a conceptual level to be the world's greatest dad. Simply be the kind of man you want your daughter to marry and your son to become. So, easy conceptually, but in execution it's harder than hell.

If you don't have kids and are contemplating divorce, just simply work through it. Or get divorced and move on. I don't care. However, if you have a child or multiple children, and if you and your wife are in that difficult place; then please read on. I can promise some wisdom borne of my trials and tribulations as a divorced dad. It just might help you through this time in your life.

Divorced Dads' Rule #2:
GET DIVORCED AS FAST AS YOU CAN.

The "Divorced Dads' Rule Number 1" will come later in the book. Hey, I wrote the book, and I can order these rules any way I want. If you don't like my numerical sequencing, then go write your own damn book.

Okay – so the title of this chapter makes it sound like I am a proponent of divorce, which is misleading. I am only a believer that when all other options have been considered and exhausted, you should get it done as fast as possible.

The process is a train wreck.

Here's the deal as I see it. If you're in a marriage that you don't want to be in, and you don't have kids, simply cut the sheets. Divide up the stuff, and move on. You're given an opportunity to manage through the remainder of your life without much, if any, interaction with your ex-spouse.

If kids are involved, it's a whole different matter entirely. My real point is once you've made the decision – move at light speed.

The process is a buzz kill.

It will take an emotional toll on both of you, and somehow, someway, that will also affect the kids. The process will drive all sorts of previously sublimated anger and frustration out of the woods, and bitter becomes the word of the day. This bitterness will definitely cause the kids some suffering. Remember through all of this to protect the kids, as they are the innocents in this dance. Also, the longer this process lasts, the higher the probability you will soil any opportunity to end this marriage amicably. I suggest to all my friends and acquaintances who are experiencing marital difficulty to go home and work it out. But if you can't work it out, the next advice I give is to get divorced as soon as possible. There is nothing healthy about the divorce process. Being married or being divorced can indeed be a healthy situation, but going through the legal and emotional upheaval of the divorce process takes a toll on everyone. It's far more emotionally draining than the wedding process. I mean, come on, picking china patterns and stemware? That was like eating glass, and you know it. But the divorce process is a shit sandwich.

If you have kids, and your biggest strife is money-related; go figure out how much easier it's going to be with an additional house note as well as child support. Still want to get unhitched because of money?

If sex is the critical issue, then go figure out what it's going to be like spending most of your nights alone over the coming years. Of course, this is after you have a go at that doxy that we recently divorced guys always seem to go after.

Divorce doesn't grant financial freedom. For most of us, it adds to the cost of living. If you have children with this woman, you can bet you will have however many years left, until your kid turns eighteen, to continue to deal with the challenges your ex-wife brings to the relationship. Does that make you sweat? It should. Because it's an undeniable truth. But not to worry, because you will put her through the same grinding bullshit in raising the kids that you did as a husband. Don't think for a moment that just because you are divorced, you won't have to put up with her stuff, and again, she yours. As the thing that drives you most nuts about this woman will continue to drive you nuts as you co-parent these kids into their young adulthood.

More on this later.

Divorced Dads' Rule #3:
**CAVE IN ON EVERYTHING THAT IS NOT LIFE
CHANGING.**

You may find yourselves – I know we did – in a situation where you are arguing over scraps.

Look – be the rational thinker, and cave in. Give in on everything, give in on anything…well, almost anything. The whole idea is to move the process forward. Give in on everything that is not life changing. The value of most things is not worth (a) paying the attorneys any more or (b) the ill will which you are creating. This is a very big consideration and the driver behind "Divorced Dad's Rule Number 3".

Look – I don't know what "life-changing" money is for you. But for me, it seemed to be anything that I couldn't make back over a few years of hard work. I'll bet that probably seems expensive, but arguing tooth and nail over those items will only exacerbate the ill will your ex-wife will have. And I can tell you for certain it's going to revisit you in coming years as you try to co-parent.

No amount of money is worth emotionally banging the kids around. Be the bigger man. Fold your hand early. Eat that glass for the kids.

Hey – a warning – if there is some material item you truly cherish, don't walk away without it, even if it comes at an expensive price. There's a reason for that emotional attachment. I don't know what is it, but you've got a reason. That emotional attachment is valid, whatever the reason may be, unless of course, it is being driven by your desire that she not have the item.

For me, this was one of the antique rugs we had on our den floor. My wife didn't particularly care for the rug, and man, I had great memories of playing and wrestling with my kids on that rug. It meant something to me. And while obviously I've moved past it over these twelve years, I still have fond memories of reading and wrestling on that old rug. You know, in retrospect, I would have negotiated more for the rug; then the kids and I could have continued to make memories on the rug.

If it's important to you, try to work it into the deal.

But look, above all else, keep the kids in mind and out of harm's way. They are the innocents. There's probably a storm of emotions going on when you're not around. This whole divorce drives a lot of failure emotions in the woman's mind. The havoc brought on by the fear of being on their own will drive plenty of spiraling negative emotions in any woman. I believe, that regardless of how strong a woman she is, she will be scared. I was, too, a bit. This is due to the fact that her new shoes are not the ones she's been programmed to wear (especially if she wasn't looking for a change of shoes). Look – this may not be such a politically correct statement, but hey – I believe that most of us are programmed with that romantic ideal of life (and women especially so). Romantic notions and fairytales seldom end at the courthouse with the striking of a judge's gavel.

I'm not trying to be sexist here or judgmental at all. Hey – give her a break. She's got her baggage, and you've got yours, and I've got mine. Always remember, if you feel like you're losing in these negotiations, just go home and look in your kids' eyes. Surely your loss may be their win. And look, it should go without saying, don't be bitter once the deal is cut. Just move on. One bitter parent is one too many for the kids to have to deal with.

Divorced Dads' Rule #4:
**TELLING THE KIDS IS FAR MORE EMOTIONAL
ON YOU THAN IT IS ON THEM.**

Hey – this is an "age-specific" lesson. My guys were little bitty, three and five, when our marriage ended. I don't know how to tell middle school kids or teenagers about the break up of their family. I've been told, and I've experienced with my children's friends, that this is probably a tougher conversation.

Regardless of the age, what you are discussing with your children is a change of shoes. Now I'm not implying that it's as simple as that, but just using "changing shoes" as an analogy. These shoes are new, and they're uncomfortable. They are going to take some time to "break-in". All the kids need to know, and all the kids want to know, is they are loved. They are not at fault, and their life is going to be okay. Mom and dad may not live in the same house, but they both still love the kids very much and that part will not change. Once the kiddos come to understand that the love is still there, they will only have to deal with the logistics of two homes. But until they get used to that change, you can expect some kind of inappropriate behavior. Hey, relax into that. Nurture them, and don't make it any more difficult on them than it already is. Fear and misplaced guilt will dissipate once these kids are comfortable they will be okay in life. Hey – it takes time to break in new shoes.

When it came time to tell our little children the news that mommy and daddy weren't going to be married anymore, we decided to rehearse the conversation. The rehearsals went along fine; but as we got ready to tell the kids, my wife said, "And I'm going to tell them that you want the divorce".

"Oh hell", I said. "We just went through this! We're going to tell them we have talked about this, and we have decided we are going to get a divorce. And then I'm going to tell them we both love them an awful lot."

We put off the conversation that day because we couldn't agree on that one point. We actually had another false start for the same reasons. I didn't want my children hearing that their daddy wanted to divorce their mommy. There was plenty of time in the future to go through all of that, but it didn't seem to me to be pertinent at that point. Maybe I was being defensive and scared that they would fault me for everything. I don't know. But I didn't want to go into it then.

You know, in retrospect, I believe they heard that very line at some point later in the next week or month or perhaps repeatedly over the years. You can't control what goes on in mom's house any more than she can control what goes on in your house.

Let go and enjoy the ride.

The kids will figure it all out over time. Don't fight unnecessary ego-charged battles in front of or at the expense of the innocents. The kids will form whatever opinions early in the new dance, and over time they will reform their opinions of you based upon how you choose to live your life and how you choose to parent – opinions based upon what kind of man you choose to be. They will come to understand what kind of man you are and what you stand for.

Simply, be a good man!

After all, you have had opinions about your parents at different stages of your development. If your folks are good people, then you came to realize that at some point. Your children will come to the same conclusion.

That is – I'm assuming you are a good man.

Finally, the moment came to tell our wee ones about the change of lifestyle that was approaching. My wife insisted we use the Mister Rogers "Talks About Divorce" or whatever the hell the name of the book was. I even recall glossing over a copy of "When Dinosaurs Divorce". Can you imagine that title? I don't know. I guess I was wrong all along thinking that it was a meteor that spelled their doom. Now I realize they didn't procreate because they all got divorced!

Well, we sat our kiddos down on the floor in the den, and we sat with them. I told them that mommy and daddy were going to get a divorce and that daddy was going to a new home, and they would now live with mommy in this house and daddy in the new house. This comment was met with total silence.

Hey – so far so good I thought.

I then said that mommy wanted me to read a book from Mister Rogers about what happens when parents get divorced. I opened the book and began. You know, at some point in this book, it says, "Now, don't think that it's your fault".

At that very point, my three year old son stood up, looked me directly in the eye, and said, "Do you want a divorce?"

"Ya," I replied.

Then he turned to his mom and said, "Do you want a divorce?"

"Yes," she responded.

He went further, "If you want a divorce", pointing at me, "and you want a divorce", pointing at his mom, "and I don't want a divorce, how can it be my fault?"

I laughed and said, "You're right, bud, let's go get some ice cream!"

And we did.

The point to that story is that my wife and I were all wound up about this conversation. These guys were little, and they had no concept of divorce. They didn't think a day ahead in their lives, and this conversation had no impact. It was all about futures. It's a reminder of how we, as adults, can build things up in our minds to be far, far greater in the moment than they could ever be for a kid.

Look – tell them you love them, and move on. They'll come to know what being kids of divorce means over time. And they will come to understand what kind of parent you choose to be by your actions over time. They're not going to get this through one conversation about a failed marriage or Fred Rogers' book.

God bless Fred Rogers.

Divorced Dads' Rule #5:
**THAT WHICH MOST DRIVES YOU CRAZY ABOUT
YOUR WIFE WILL CONTINUE TO DRIVE YOU
CRAZY AS YOU RAISE CHILDREN.**

Here's the deal. All that your ex-wife did as your wife that drove you nuts will continue throughout the co-parenting years. All of that manipulation, conscious or unconscious, is gonna continue. By the way, everything you did to drive her to distraction in the marriage will also drive her nuts as you co-parent. This, I guess, is your only revenge. These are adult patterns, and this dynamic takes a long time to rectify. And this assumes both divorcees are willing to change and willing to put in the effort. Not very realistic, I might add. Reminds me of the old joke: "How many shrinks does it take to change a light bulb? Only one! But the light bulb's gotta' wanna' change."

In my life, this manipulative behavior has been an ongoing source of frustration. And every time I feel like I've got a handle on my reactions to my ex-wife's manipulation, I get crossways and frustrated all over again. And be sure, she is unconsciously competent at this manipulation. And why wouldn't she be? I've co-trained her to be great at it. Look, this isn't to bash my ex- in any way, shape, or form. I could just as easily be talking about my manipulative manners. In our case, I can be controlling and try to dominate the direction and outcome of conversations and events. You know – I guess I might be one of those guys who feels like anybody who agrees with him is pretty damn smart, and anyone who disagrees with him is pretty damn dumb. This is not my most highly acclaimed personality trait. But it's probably true as often as not.

My kids' mom, on the other hand, has mastered being passive-aggressive with me. She's taken it to an art form; and quite honestly, I've helped train her to be such a samurai. Every dance has two partners. In our marriage, this dynamic was brought about at times when I would express dissatisfaction with one of her actions. I'd tell her that whatever she did made me feel a certain way – less than, or less loved, or less respected, whatever. She'd respond by turning on the waterworks. Man, her tears were very real, and the sobbing would lock me up as fast as you can possibly imagine. Part of my personality at the time, anyway, was I didn't ever want to hurt or make the person I loved cry. I'd shut down that conversation, and she'd eventually stop crying. And we would all be at peace – issues unresolved but no more raised blood pressure.

It was a brilliantly executed unconscious dance on our part. I never realized until it was far too late we were living in a world where issues were never resolved. This is not a healthy place for a man or a woman. Once divorced, I began to realize her mastery of this passive-aggressive manipulation of me; and frankly, my willingness to participate in that dance came at the detriment of our kids.

An example of this comes in a story, which quite frankly, is the most difficult time I have had in parenting or co-parenting. My son was placed by his mom on drugs to control ADHD. However, my son had never been officially diagnosed as having ADHD. "Borderline" was the term used, and the drugs were recommended to help him with his situation. I won't go into the whole argument about Ritalin kids and the fact that 25% of all public school nine year old boys are diagnosed with ADHD. With a statistic like that, I would argue *most* nine year old boys exhibit borderline tendencies. So we drug these kids. You know, the stats for nine year old girls are dramatically different. So I guess they're saying this syndrome is Y chromosome related and is best dealt with a daily dose of amphetamines, at least according to the medical field and a few pill pushing pharmaceutical companies. Hey – don't get me started on that B.S.! Do you sometimes think that the pharmaceutical companies won't rest until we are all popping at least one pill a day? Look, my suggestion is join'em, don't fight'em. Go buy pharmaceutical stocks!

My ex-wife and I struggled mightily with the conversations around putting our son on drugs. I was adamant that until he was diagnosed we wouldn't even consider drugs. I also contended that if diagnosed, we should exhaust all other potential remedies: change of diet, change of school, more rigor around parenting, and potentially, a decrease in video games as I'd read some article tying some of the behavior to an over-abundance of video game playing. You reach for anything at times like this. You know, in retrospect, I figure that the decrease in video game playing would have really just been part of the change of behavior and more rigor around parenting. We went around and around on this, and the

18

conversation was emotionally filled from both sides and never resolved. Hey – I was not completely ruling out that our son could be ADHD or that drugs could help him. I was simply suggesting, and rather adamantly, that we try all other solutions before we began his day with an upper. The conversations were heated, and both of us turned to our attorneys for a better idea of our respective options and potential outcomes here.

I thought the issue would never die down as there never seemed to be an end to the argument. And then one day, my ex-wife simply stopped arguing. I didn't realize it at the time, but she had completely stopped talking about this or any other subject other than the divorced parent's logistical conversations over when and where to pick up and drop off the kids, etc. Months passed, I thought we were out of the woods on this one. One day while hanging out at our house, my son let it slip, unconsciously wanting to or unconsciously needing to, that he was taking a pill every day and that he had been doing so for a long time. He went on to say that his sister knew about it, and both were instructed by their mother not to tell daddy. I was outraged. I felt violated, but most of all I felt completely out of control with regard to protecting my children. I called my attorney the very next day, and I explained to him what happened. He calmly told me we could pursue this in court, as this was definitely in violation of the divorce decree which stated that any non-emergency medications would be given only with the consent of both parents. I asked him to explain how we would go forward with shutting this down. His response chilled me to the bone. "Well, we go to court, and we get your kids up in front of a judge to talk about what their mom did."

Wow! She won damn it! She won. I would never get my kids to speak out against their mom. I'm screwed and so is my son. That's all I could think of. This story to this day is not a great memory. The only good news out of any of this is that my son no longer takes meds.

As you listen to this story, you may boldly declare you would have nailed her to the wall on this one. And perhaps that could have or should have been done by me. The point of the story is not that my ex-wife is some witch. Hell! I believe she was completely convinced that what she was doing was best for her child. It was simply (did I say simply?) a matter of us being diametrically opposed on the how-to of a very emotionally-charged parenting challenge. Now this example is used to illustrate how a dynamic, a dance if you will, that began in marriage or more probably in courtship, spilled over into our co-parenting roles. Or better put in the beginning of this chapter, Divorced Dads' Rule #5: "That which drives you most crazy about your ex-wife will continue to drive you crazy as you raise your children."

Divorced Dads' Rule #6:
GO GET LAID!

The dating game should be played with integrity. Because believe me, the kids are watching. And they see everything.

Hey – go out and get you some! Look, you're single and you want to get laid. Come on, admit it. You've been thinking about this for a long time. You think it's going to make things better. So go ahead. It won't make any difference, but you think it will. So go get you some. Feel free to go out with whomever you want.

While I'm on the subject of adult dating, well, I wish you the best of luck, 'cause you're going to need it. It's with some trepidation that I write this chapter, as I'm no expert on dating. I do, however, have lots of experience over the past 12 years of being a single man. I could speak to dating a ton, and even falling in love twice over that period. All of these experiences have shed some light on how to get the kids through the dating process without leaving too much damage to their perception of healthy relationships.

So back to it. Go get laid. Get with that young doxy at the neighborhood bar or wherever. Get on the internet match finding services. Go ahead. Get it over with. Go find that first fling you've been fantasizing about since you contemplated being a single man. Chances are it won't last too long, and chances are you'll be attracted to her for all the wrong reasons.

There's an entire book that could be written on the polarity swapping we do once we come out of a relationship. Let me give you an example. Your ex-wife wasn't passionate at all so you go find the most passionate woman you've ever known. Well, chances are you were attracted to your wife for some reasons that may still exist, although probably no longer with her. And the most passionate woman whom I ever encountered turned out to be a bit of a wack-job.

By the way, this is not a psychology or self-help book so go find one if you need it. Or go find a shrink to help you recognize and deal with your polarity swapping. The point is that polarity swapping is very common. It is to be expected until you recognize it and until you get a handle on it. Any woman who is the exact opposite of the last woman is probably not the answer to your relationship questions. She is most probably just a breath of fresh air that will soon enough peter out. Most of them won't last probably because that opposite attraction, that polarity swapping, is not sustainable energy. It's got no legs.

The only caution at this point is to not integrate that first fling into your children's lives, or better yet, maybe not the first few ladies. This can be tough. You'll be excited with all the energy associated with the new and seemingly sexier woman in your life. However, hold off. Hold her off from the kiddos as it is better for the kids because the first one is most probably going to flame out. Now that doesn't mean you shouldn't go after the fun, but just protect the kids from your inability to make conscious healthy choices for you and for them. Hey – being single is like wearing new shoes. You're bound to get a blister or two as you stumble through the dance. Don't blister the kids.

And speaking of blisters – wrap that rascal!

The first woman with whom you engage could come in a variety of sizes and shapes, but you can probably bet it will be a clear case of polarity swapping. Polarity swapping would best be described as finding that which is everything your former spouse is not. My first relationship after my divorce was with the Uber-outdoorswoman. My ex-wife would let me follow my passion of being outside as much as I wanted. Hey – credit to her for that. Trips to the mountains, and rivers, and camera safaris were something that fed my soul. My ex-wife, on the other hand, preferred malls, movies, and air conditioning. She did, however, allow me to get my fill without giving me grief over it. Now a litany could be written on how we paired up, but this book is about life and raising kids after divorce. I don't have the stamina to write a book about how relationships begin, what it takes to keep them going, or why they flame out. Go to the self-help books or Dr. Phil to get some quick answer on the human condition – not here.

Back to the first woman. The first woman I dated after my divorce was full of energy, and she had a great zest to live life to the fullest.

"Living is not about flat-lining!" she would say.

24

She loved the blues, and she enjoyed dancing to the wee hours in a dark, dingy blues joint. She was up for anything as long as that music was moving, and man could she ever move. She was a fitness freak and loved to go whitewater rafting. We worked out together, we danced together, and we ran the Grand Canyon's rapids in two person oar rafts. Life was exhilarating with her. It was a great first experience in the world of adult relationships.

She once told me, "I love dating you recently divorced guys. Ya'll are so easy to please. You've been pent up for so long that just a little affection goes a long way."

This relationship was fun, and it lasted for a handful of months. Now, the lady was not what I ultimately wanted in a partner, and I was probably not what she wanted long term. This was a fact which we both discovered over a few intense months. She was intent on gulping down life, and the notion of ever slowing down wasn't in her immediate or long term game plan. Hey – power to her! For me, it seemed that this lifestyle, with two kids no less, was not going to feed my soul. If I did spend an extended period of time with her, there would need to be more substance to our relationship. Hell – there would need to be some substance to our relationship! What was needed was something other than the fact that she was the exact opposite of my ex-wife. We parted on great terms as adults should. When I see her, we both have great memories of time well spent.

Years later, I fell in love with a woman. She made a comment that struck me to the core. She was recently divorced. Actually, as I recall, she was not even final with the paperwork, but she had been separated for some time. One sweet calm evening she said, "You are nothing like my ex-husband."

Man – I was shocked. I thought for 30 seconds, and then I responded. "Wait. Wait a minute. I know Bob. And we're actually very much alike. Yep. I can be more serious and focused on a life plan than him, but we're both extremely gregarious. We love to be the jokester at the party, and we both have a pretty goofy sense of humor. He's a good man with a gentle heart and full of life. I am that too."

I really loved this woman, and I gave in an unhealthy manner to keep this relationship afloat. She may have also. Perhaps, as divorced adults, we somehow unconsciously felt this was our last shot – our last shot at relationship bliss. It was not the case.

That relationship went away, and she's gone off to become a married woman. From what I've heard from her and others, she's happy in her choices. I've moved on over the years and dated on a pretty frequent basis and even fallen in love once more. Neither of those loves gave me a life partner, but both have taught me life lessons I can utilize to become a better man. And both have taught me life lessons I can share with my children. It took me some time to realize these first two relationships were clear cases of polarity swapping – me with another (the Uber-outdoorswoman) or the other with me (the woman who saw me as the exact opposite of her ex-husband). In these first two "post divorce" relationships, I was dancing the dance of polarity swapping. Certainly, it was an unsustainable dance indeed. Neither of those relationships had legs, and both petered out over time. There's no regret in either of these stories. The only thing I would change is I probably wouldn't have exposed my kids to the first relationships as much as I did. For if I could have better understood at the time what was going on unconsciously within me, I might have been better able to shield my children from my unconscious actions. It might have been healthier for my children if I could have better understood that the first dating situation was more about what I was moving away from and less about what I was moving towards. The second relationship where I had fallen in love was about what she was moving away from more than what she was moving towards.

Further, I can look back on multiple short-term relationships that came and went before the seasons changed. In each case my kids, after the demise of those relationships, experienced some form of loss. They had someone come into their world and share laughter and grant attention. They had someone come into their world and bring smiles to their dad's face. In the end, the relationships were to prove short-term, as they were built on shifting sand. Surely, surely my kids experienced some loss.

I've experienced dating women who have their own children, and those who are not parents. The experiences have proven as varied as the women. The experiences have also proven as emotionally healthy as the women. Typically, I've found that mothers have a better understanding of what time requirements are involved in being a parent. Now that makes for an understanding dating partner. However, the logistics of two parents dating can get pretty daunting. It turns into a matter of matching calendars to find time together alone. This can be exacerbated, as I have experienced before, if you have opposite custody schedules. If her kids are with her when you are without yours, then you are either apart or taking up some of her quality time with her children or vice versa. Dating a mother of more than two can create conversations like, "Okay, so we're free on Tuesday from 4:00 pm to 7:15 pm. Okay great! Let's make a date".

Regardless, the kids come first – hers and yours.

Once I was on a third date at the movies with a lady when her cell phone rang. She turned to me and whispered, "I'll be right back." She returned and told me we had to leave the movie theater. I got up, and we walked out. At the exit she said that some trouble had come up with her teen son, and she needed to get home. She began this long explanation and launched into an apology. I smiled and placed my hand on her shoulder and said, "Hey, no need. The next time it could be my kids. The kids always come first."

After her parenting crisis had subsided, she went on and on about what a considerate man I was by making things so easy for her. I felt like she was making a bigger deal out of this than was warranted. After all, what kind of man would have his own children at interest and drop and run for them at any time of need, and then not understand that reciprocity was the only true path. I told her I never wanted her to feel torn or conflicted about needing to spend time with her kids. If even at the last minute or the last second things changed and she needed to readjust or bail on our date, if it were for the kiddos, she need not give it a second thought. I surely would do that for mine. If you can't step up to the plate on this, then you shouldn't date women with kids. And if the woman you are dating can't step up to this, then you should move on down the road.

Additionally, if you're dating a woman with children, and you're trying to get time together, you may choose to jam those kids together. You might figure, "Hey, she's got a little girl. And I've got a little girl. They can be play buddies." My experience tells me that with the little ones this is possible. But as the kids move past, I don't know....age 8 or 9, they may not want to be jammed together with some kid whose only common denominator is the parents' mutual attraction for one another. Give the kids a break. Remember when your mom would have one of her friends come over, and you were told to go in the backyard and play with her friend's son Osgood? This would inevitably come at the same time as when your best buddy would call to invite you over to spend the night. Sucked to be you, pal.

Yep, give the kids a break.

I've also dated some women who don't have kids and found some to be completely understanding, and even liked and respected me more for the manner in which I prioritize parenting. I believe they saw this as the sign of a good man. However, I have dated, for very brief periods, a few women who were envious of the time and the relationship I have with my kiddos, even resentful. From these women, I suggest you run like hell. I did.

Additionally, you are the parent of yours and she of hers. Don't get into parenting or disciplining her kids, and don't allow her to do so with yours. The kids will resent it. And look, if you are being truly honest with yourself, you will resent it too. And watch out for the questioning of each other's parenting styles. That is an emotionally-charged dialogue.

Also look out for becoming an inconsistent parent in these adult dating situations. Here's the deal. You treat your kids a certain way, and you have set expectations and behavior which you have come to understand. And hopefully the kids feel comfortable with and flourish within those parameters. Along comes your new lady and you now want to show her how great your kids are. So you tighten up on the parameters of acceptable behavior. This is like throwing them a change-up. Foul! Don't change the way you parent your kids for anyone and certainly not to impress anyone. You see this all the time in public places like the grocery store.

The kids step out of line, the parents are embarrassed, and so they over-correct driven by that embarrassment. If you've not seen this or experienced it with your own kids, then you need to pay more attention. It is going on all around you. It is probably going on around you in your home. Think back to those visits to grandparents or Aunt Mabel's house. You know those homes with all those breakable knick-knacks, Lladros, or whatever the hell they are. You were on pins and needles. You were hovering over your kids the whole time. You slam them every time they look like they are going to breathe wrong. You don't want to have to replace that broken stuff, and you don't want to feel embarrassed about your kids' actions when, hey, all they're doing is being kids. All kids want, in terms of parenting, is to know they are loved and consistency – give them consistent parameters. Don't change the way you parent.

By the way, dating as an adult is very different than dating as a teen or college kid. Even if it has been since your early to mid twenties since you were last single, things have changed a bunch.

So I was at this crawfish boil and a friend of a friend was excitedly talking about her first dating experiences since the death of her husband. It seemed she and her husband had one of those good, healthy relationships – one of those great marriages to which many aspire. Now he passed a year or two ago, and she was just now dipping her toe back into the dating pool. She was excitedly discussing her quandary with all the other adults at the party (some married, some single) – but all at the same table.

She was struggling with the fact she had met this one guy in a nearby town on a recent trip back home. Her struggle was around the fact that she had also, just prior to that trip back home, gone out with some local fellow. She didn't know how to broach the subject with either of them, but she had a desire to continue seeing both of them. She feared bringing that conversation up with them, as she thought it might run one or both off.

I listened to her story, and I reached over the table to put my hand on her hand. "Ann, first I gotta tell you your radiance is shining through in your smile and in your eyes. I can see your excitement. I can feel your excitement. On this dating thing, I suggest you rock on. But you gotta realize, Ann, dating as adults is a lot different than dating as teens."

"How so? What do you mean?" she asked.

"Well, when you're an adult, you can expect the other party to own their own shit. And if they don't, you've got to cull them from your list of dating options immediately. If the guy in the first few weeks of dating you has issues with you going out with others, then he lacks confidence in himself. Additionally, a guy like that – man, he's going to show you more control issues as things go forward. Look, it's early for you in this, and you should try on as many pairs of shoes until you find a pair you want to dance in long term. You don't have to be so upfront and tell them everything or anything about dating others in the first few weeks – unless they ask. Then tell them what's what."

Another way adult dating is different than teen or college dating is that adults come with baggage. Typically, lots of baggage. Teen and college-age dating can be wrapped up in all the drama associated with those tumultuous times. If you're dating an adult, you'd better be prepared to have more patience and do a bit of tongue-biting because she has her stuff. And by the way, so do you.

If you're looking for a partner, then I suggest you look to the core. If it is good to the core, then the rest is perhaps just noise. If you bail every time you see something in a woman that is evidence she has been scarred up emotionally, then you will have lots of first dates… and a lot of last dates, too.

Oh, and use condoms, and insist on mutual HIV tests. It's worth it for the kids, even if you seem to be willing to play roulette with anyone who has ever slept with anyone who has ever slept with anyone, etc. Playing 6 degrees of HIV or STD separation is not my idea of good lifestyle choice. Given the odds, I'd still rather win the lottery.

Ultimate advice on dating with kids would be to protect the kids and keep them out of the rebound. Keep them out of the polarity swapping or casual relationships, and only bring them around once you have decided you want this person in your life for more than a month or two.

Additionally, don't sleep with her while the kids are in house. What kind of morals do you want your kids to grow up with? There are plenty of times to get your "ya-ya's" with the lady when the kids aren't around. This is big important advice, as the kids – man, they're observing everything. I can recall my 17 year old daughter giving me grief about the fact that my lady love slept in a different bedroom when my kids were around. I told her I'd made a decision long ago not to be the kind of man who slept with women in front of his kids. She said that was weird and laughed at me. I wanted to further defend my actions, and then I just thought better of it. I believe she was testing me, and in time, she and her brother will respect the fact that at least in our house, we showed some moral fiber.

At the risk of beating a dead horse, and repeating myself too much, I suggest that it's a best practice not to bring around the ones that aren't going to last. I cannot say I executed well on this guideline, but in retrospect, I wish I'd have handled it differently. My kids have met and spent time with many ladies I dated, casually or otherwise. I've been divorced for more than 12 years, and I've dated my fair share of women. There have been 2 special ladies and a few others who were high quality people. These ladies, I've got no regrets about my kids spending time with. They learned something, to be sure, from each of these women, as they were special people. It is the ladies who didn't stick around, be it my choice or theirs, from whom I could have protected my kids better. A lot better.

I kind of think the upside for my children, in this experience, is that they understand every relationships does not end in marital bliss. On the other hand, I do sometimes wonder if my kids think that *no* relationship will end in long-term commitment. I guess a decent rule of thumb may be to protect the kids from exposure from the first 6 or 7 months of any relationship, of all relationships. If the lady lasts longer than that, then she is probably someone special, special to you, and perhaps the kids should get to know her.

Finally, I can say my children have felt a pretty severe loss when one of the very special ladies in my life discontinued her dance with me. I have no real advice here, other than to talk openly and honestly with the kids about relationships ending or taking on new dynamics. There is loss associated with the end of a dance. It's a change of shoes, which sometimes is our choice and sometimes the choice of the other dance partner.

Divorced Dads' Rule #1:
NEVER UTTER A DISCOURAGING WORD ABOUT
YOUR KIDS' MOM.

If you can do this, then you're a better man than me.

Look – if I could take back every audible sigh, every roll of the eyes, every negatively inflected statement about my children's mom I have ever made in front of the kids, I'd gladly do so. I made it a point, and I still do, to not bash their mom in front of the kids. But over the years, I've shown to be weak or petty at times, and they know I often disagree with their mom's choices in life and in parenting. There's no upside in doing this as the kids will only get defensive. For God's sake, she's their mom. And they will go to battle silently or outright with you over this. I mean "what the hell!" How defensive do you get when somebody bashes your mom? Bad execution around this, and they may grow up with disrespect for their mom. After all, that is what they've observed from the man who's supposed to show them the way. Set the example and never let them see you sweat. Never utter a discouraging word about her.

Eat that glass for the kids.

If you will do this, there's a pretty fair chance you will be your children's only parent to do so. It's also a good bet that your ex-wife will have resentment for you over the divorce, and it will spill over. You did, after all, help to shatter that romantic notion of "happily ever after". She may also have bitterness or be fearful over the fact that financially you will most likely improve your standard of living, and she will not. Hey – I'm no male chauvinist pig here, but there's simply too much data supporting this fact. If indeed your ex-wife exercises her resentment in a manner that causes her to bash dad in front of the kids, you've got to let it go. Eat that glass for the kids. When they hear it, the kids will believe it; and you aren't going to change their minds when they're really small. She is their mommy after all. To confront your ex- in that moment is to basically call mom a liar. Look, eat the glass and move on. Over time, they'll come to understand what kind of man you are; and that's your blessing (or your curse) depending on what kind of man you choose to be.

You know, in my situation, my kids have heard for years how mom never has any money. I didn't know it, but for a very long time, perhaps seven years or so after we were divorced, my kids didn't even know that every month their dad wrote a child support check to their mom – and a fairly hefty check at that. I didn't turn that into a negative event but rather told them I'd been doing so and would continue to do so without fail or interruption until they were adults. I believed then and I believe now that over time they'll begin to understand who was telling which stories and for what reasons. Time has proven me correct on this issue, and it's made me resolute that this should be **Rule #1: Never utter a discouraging word about your children's mom.**

Hey look – the kids are the innocents here. There's no need to screw them up any more than you're going to anyway. They're probably going to end up on a shrink's couch someday to be sure, but don't give them this as a reason. Be a man. They'll thank you for it later, and you'll have less glass to eat as you'll be raising healthier teens. Think of it as an investment. It may take a while, and they may not realize you walked with integrity until they are well into adulthood. Hell! You may not even live long enough to see it. But they will come to this understanding, and they will be the better for it and so will their offspring and the rest of the planet. Go do something good for the planet, and keep your comments to yourself.

If you need to vent, pick one friend and whine away to him or her. I suggest this not be a family member. Your family has already sided with you, and any more negativity associated with your children's mother is only going to come out around your kids or when your ex-wife encounters your family at the kiddos' functions. I'd also suggest you keep it to only one or two friends as opposed to everyone in your circle. Because I have to tell you, eventually, you will wear them all out. If you do so, you'll probably end up alienating at least one of these friends with your whining. They didn't marry her, and they don't want to deal with her or your baggage any more than they have to.

Above all else, it might be wise to realize the more you trash your ex-wife, the goofier you look for ever choosing her to begin with. Be a better man. And if it helps, every time you think you're getting the short end of the stick, know that in time your kids will get it. They will get who you are. Hey – eventually you did with your parents. Eventually, they will with you.

Divorced Dads' Rule #7:
YOUR EX-WIFE'S FRIENDS AND FAMILY WON'T
BE YOUR FRIENDS AND FAMILY.

Hey – they won't like you. So don't waste your time or effort on that goal.

Now this rule seems like it shouldn't even be something you have to consider. But it will no doubt come up, as your kids may be friends with your ex-wife's friends' kids. It will take some patience with these folks, as they are probably only hearing one side of the story. And you can bet your ass it isn't your side! Not such a big deal when you think about it because you're probably telling your buddies a pretty one-sided story when you talk about your ex. Once again, be a man. Take the high road with these folks. Have patience with them. Have patience with them for your children. Eat that glass for your kids. Those folks may come up with some pretty bizarre behavior when they encounter you.

So here's a story to exemplify.

My kiddos' birthdays fall on consecutive months. We would always, and sometimes still do, have individual parties with my big ol' goofy family. And on most years, when they were young, their mom would have a party for them and their friends at her house, and I'd put together a party at my house. It's not such a tough break for divorced kids to have all these parties thrown in their honor. About a year after the divorce, I called all my ex-wife's friends who had kids and invited them over to a party for my children. Now we lived across town from all these people, so my sister and I volunteered for bus duty. We both had big SUVs, and I figured, hey, that's about the only way we can assure high attendance for my kiddo's party. One lady, God bless you Miss Patty.....wherever you are, said she thought it was nuts and that we didn't need to drive all the way out there, pick up kids, drive back to the party, and then return the kids afterwards. She volunteered to relieve my sister. Hey, what a gal Miss Patty is.

One of my ex-wife's friends had two kids, a girl and a boy, close to my son's and daughter's age. I called them up, and the wife said, "Uh, I'd better let you talk to my husband."

He got on the phone and said, "Yeah, my kids can come. But you don't need to pick them up. I want to drive them over there and talk to them about what it means to be a child from a broken home.

I want to tell them it isn't just about getting two bikes or two of everything."

I said, "Look, that'd be great, man. And by the way, you're welcome to stay and knock down a beer or two while the kids jump on that moonwalk thing."

He came back sharply, "Look Pat. My wife and I don't like at all what you've done to your family. But I'll bring the kids because we love your children, and my kids love your children."

Wow! Just remember to breathe I thought. Just breathe.

"Sounds great! We'll start around 2:00 pm, and we'll have some grilled burgers and some beers, and we'll play some birthday games. I look forward to seeing ya'll there."

I mistakenly told my siblings about this phone call. Look – after you've been divorced a while, you pretty much quit talking about every negative scenario. You realize that bringing that kind of stuff up in front of your family only makes them defensive of you and your kids. It's bad energy. Let it go. But I was still a newbie, and these divorce shoes were fresh. My younger sister, who is one tough nut, came out with both guns blazing. She shouted, "I can't wait to see that jerk at the party! I'm going to let him know a thing or two about his bullshit."

"Hey, hey, chill out," I said. "Look – this guy's going to be a guest in my home. The party's for the kids. This house is about love and peace. You start any stuff with that guy, and I'm going to ask you to leave. Besides, if you really want to feel revenge, then talk nice to him and secretly know that his old lady has been talking to my ex-wife for a year about divorcing his ass because he doesn't make enough money."

Frankly, these confidences were way out of line for me to share with anyone. This was somebody else's personal business. But that guy had ticked me off, and he put me on the defensive. That party went on without a hitch. And the kids had a great time. As far as I'm concerned, anytime you have 25 kids at your house, and nobody gets knocked out during the piñata ordeal, that's a sign of a good party.

Her friends are not going to be your friends. Her friends are never going to be your friends. Someone like Miss Patty may surprise you and extend an olive branch. But her friends don't need to be your buddies. Kill them with kindness, and eat that glass for your kids.

Divorced Dads' Rule #8:
DON'T HIT YOUR KIDS.

Seems like a pretty simple rule, but I'm still amazed how many folks believe you can spoil the child by sparing the rod.

What the hell are we trying to teach our kids? Are we trying to show them that authority figures have the right to physically control underlings? Are we trying to teach them that might makes right.....that someone who outweighs someone else by 100 pounds has the upper hand in any confrontation? Are we trying to show them that physical altercations are the solution to our frustration? Surely when you hit your kids, you've exhausted all other means of exerting influence toward their inappropriate behavior. What are we trying to show them? Are we trying to show them we love them by hitting them? When you think about how this stuff can be perceived by a little kid, with little kid notions of right and wrong, it seems pretty easy to me to understand that no good teaching comes from hitting a kid.

When my son was about three, we found ourselves in our SUV on a road trip. He was acting like a little shit. I was tired of driving, and I was tired of dealing with his whining. I finally had enough, and I snapped. I reached to the back seat, and I swatted his leg. Hey, look, this is not one of my prouder parenting moments, as it was all born of frustration with the situation and with him. He started to cry like I'd stuck him with a branding iron. He cried on and on, for what seemed like an eternity. Finally I turned back to him, and I said, "What can I do to get you to stop crying?"

He looked at me with tears rolling down those big round cheeks; and he said, "Well, you could quit hitting me for one thing!"

Wow! Out of the mouths of babes, eh?

"Well, I guess you're probably right on that one," I said rather resolutely. I felt like a piece of trash, and I've never hit that guy since. I mean, think about it from his side. I was fried with the whole drive, and I was just plain worn out. And I'm supposed to be the adult. This little guy was not only sitting in the SUV for that long trip but also strapped to a kid's car seat, which can't be too damn comfortable. He was worn out too.

So here's the deal. Don't hit your kids, ever. Sometimes kids can be pretty great at telling you why they're acting out. If you can just maintain the calm and ask questions in a calm tone, they may be able to enlighten you.

Now my daughter was two when we brought my son home from the hospital. She had been queen bee in our house from the day she arrived, and the fact that she was the first female grandchild only added to the attention she got from my big ol' goofy family.

The first week my son was home, my wife told me our daughter had bitten our new baby boy on the hand. I took my daughter up to her room and sat down with her, and we talked about what had happened and that biting people was not allowed. A few days later she bit him again. I was flustered as hell. And I took her up to her room again, and I made her put all of her dolls in a box. I told her I was going to take her dolls away for a week, and I was going to leave that doll-filled box on her dresser so she could see it every day as a reminder that biting was bad stuff. Frankly, in retrospect, this is probably not great parenting. I don't know, but I was new to the game and I was still finding my way.

It happened a third time. Man, I was exasperated as hell. We went to her room, and we sat down on the bed one more time. I told her we had already talked about this twice and that I had taken her dolls away, and I was sure she knew biting was bad. I then said, "Baby, I can't figure this one out. I need your help. I need for you to tell me why, why you keep biting your brother, even when you know biting is wrong."

She looked up at me with those crystalline blue eyes of hers, and she said, "Daddy, I used to get all of the attention. Now he gets all the attention. I know biting is bad and all, and I know that the attention I get is bad attention, but at least I'm getting attention."

I was floored. This kid was two years old, and she could articulate, when given the chance, exactly what was causing her to act out in such a negative manner. I hugged her, and I said, "I love you. Your mommy loves you. We have a world of love in our hearts, and we will never love him more than we love you, and we will never love you more than we love him. We love you both equally.

People's ability to love is huge, and we have enough love in our hearts to love you and your brother a lot."

I got up and got the boxed-up dolls off the dresser, and I put them on the bed next to her. Then I added, "Sweetie, I'm giving you all your dolls back. I feel like if I had asked you before why you were doing this biting thing, you would have told me. I understand what you said about attention and everything. I have to tell you I think you're the most incredible kid I've ever been around. Heck, most adults can't tell you why they do bad stuff. But you're only two years old, and you know why, and you can even tell me why. You are an incredible little girl!"

Then I told her, "Baby-Habey, if you ever feel like you aren't getting mommy's or daddy's attention the way you need it, just stop us, and ask us for it! Just say, 'Hey, I need some attention here!' And we will stop whatever we are doing, and give you some good attention. We want you to feel as loved as we love you."

Hugs followed that moment. The biting stopped. Crisis resolved. Order restored.

From that moment on, I can recall many occasions where my daughter would blurt out, completely out of the blue, and even at some inappropriate times, "Hey, I need some attention!" At other times she might say, "So when are we going to talk about me?"

When faced with perplexing parenting situations, it may indeed be a good thing to sit down with your child in a safe, quiet place, and in a calm voice, ask them what's going on with them. Don't just make the assumptions. You might be surprised, as I was, to learn they can help you become a better parent.

Divorced Dads' Rule #9:
GO FIND A CHILD REARING MENTOR.

Man – my kids were fortunate that my older sister was a bit ahead of the curve in the whole child rearing game.

I didn't realize early on that she'd be such a powerful, powerful influence on how I'd raise my children. My sister's kids are a handful of years ahead, age-wise, from my guys. My kiddos and I are very, very blessed to have them in our lives.

Now, I didn't consciously go out and find a mentor. She became mine in an elegant and developmental manner over several years. I'd seek her support when times got hard. She'd offer her opinion, and usually I'd take it. Over the years we kind of became mentors to one another. And I would like to think that my counsel helped her sort through some of her child rearing challenges. But whatever gifts I gave her in no way come close to repaying all the patience, "in your face" honesty, and moral fiber which she lent to my child rearing endeavors. I found the right mentor for me, and she found the perfect person to mentor.

She's a remarkably strong woman. She's stronger than garlic. She's a woman of great integrity and fortitude. She also knows me very well and can see through all my B.S. She has plenty of faith in our mutual love and respect to hold the mirror up and challenge me when she feels I'm not being completely honest or living with authenticity or acting with integrity.

Hey – go find yourself a mentor such as her. It is a huge gift you can give to your children and to yourself.

Now in my mind, it helped that she was female. Something for you to consider, as it gives the other side of the coin perspective, right? But a strong male mentor could be of tremendous value as well. I'd listen to her speak of her child rearing beliefs, and at times mine were contrary to hers. I'd look to see the effect of some of her decisions on her kids, and I'd mirror her actions with my own. At other times, I'd disagree with her approach, and I'd take notes as to how I'd handle it differently with my kids.

Now, I've had mentors in the business world, and I've had mentors in my competitive sports world. The single greatest mentor in my life has been my sister, Suzanne. Go get you one. Your kids will be better off for it. And to be selfish about it, you'll have an easier time raising kids with some moral and directional balancing through your mentor's guidance.

Divorced Dads' Rule #10:
GIVE THE GIFTS TO THE KIDS.

Now I have heard this story told and retold by divorced parents time and time again.

Early in our divorced days, my kids and I were getting ragged on by their mom over the toys and clothes being left at my house. Her take on the situation was that she bought those clothes and bought some of those toys, and they didn't belong at my house rather they belonged at her house. I can understand this, as things were more important to her than they were to me, and truthfully, she did dress them at her house in nicer clothes than they wore at my house. But at least on your end, when you give the kids something, make sure they understand it is theirs. Make sure they understand that the gift can end up wherever they want the gift to end up. The house may belong to the parents, but the kids' gifts belong to the kids.

I can tell you there have been times when I got frustrated at my son or daughter when they would say, "Hey, I'm bored. There's nothing to do around here." This was especially frustrating when they had just gotten a haul of toys from me or my family members, but those toys were all at mom's house.

I was often compelled to say, "If you wouldn't take all that stuff to your mom's and leave it there, then you'd have the stuff to play with here." But the reality was that I, and my family, had gifted to the children and not to my household. This rule was a great opportunity to teach the kids about giving and giving unconditionally. After all, conditional gift-giving isn't really giving.

In reality, if the kids are bored, they will pretty well be bored wherever they are and with whatever entertainment is at their disposal. They're probably just tired and need a nap, but they don't yet understand that feeling enough to recognize those symptoms. Let the attachment or strings associated with the gifts go. It will teach your kids more about giving, which is a far greater gift than any doll or plastic racecar.

Now, perhaps on occasion, an exchange with the ex-wife of your house stuff and her house stuff may be an elegant manner to deal with this issue. But leave the kids out of that.

Again, the kids are the innocents here, so leave them out of it.

Divorced Dads' Rule #11:
EAT LOTS OF GLASS FOR YOUR KIDS.

You will have ample opportunity to do so as you co-parent.

There was one particular time when the dance between my ex-wife and me was not going extremely smooth. To add fuel to the fire, my ex-mother-in-law was all over my kid's mom about me and the way we were co-parenting. The subject of all this noise I can't even recall right now, but it was pretty heated at the time. My family got wind of those histrionics, and at one point, my dad pulled me aside and said, "Son, I don't know how you put up with that crap?"

"Man, it's easy!" I lied. "Dad, I watched you eat a ton of glass for your family. You worked three jobs most of the time just to make ends meet. As best I can tell, you hated every one of those jobs. Long ago, you showed me the way on this one. If this is the only shit sandwich I have to eat to make my kids' lives better, then I say bring on the mustard."

Divorced Dads' Rule #12:
QUALITY OVER QUANTITY IS BULLSHIT!

You'll hear lots of folks talk about quality time with their children.

Now I previously stated that when you are with your kids you must reserve enough energy to be in the moment or you will lose opportunities for enhancing your children's intellectual, spiritual, and emotional stability and growth. So to some degree, the quality statement has to be kept in mind. However, don't for a minute think that quality over quantity is the way to better parenting – and certainly not quality at the expense of quantity. Both are critical.

There are too many moments I call "in-between moments". These are ripe with opportunity for nurturing and parenting. I can't tell you how many times while driving somewhere in our SUV my kids and I would engage in some brilliant or near-brilliant conversation. These "in-between moments" are simple moments when all else in their world is still. To settle for quality time only might cause you to miss out on these moments. These times are indeed rich, and these times present learning for your children. The kids may not always be present, or you may not always be present if you cram them into quality over quantity.

You've got to be there to be there.

Divorced Dads' Rule #13:
DON'T MISS THE CHILD SUPPORT CHECKS – EVER!

This should not even *need* to be said.

You've made a commitment to pay child support. You've made a commitment to your ex-wife. You've made a commitment to your children. This is a commitment signed and sealed in the courts. Your children's mom will no doubt be counting on these checks to make ends meet. She will budget around these checks. If you miss or are late, you've screwed her world up as well as failed to live up to your commitments.

Believe me – if you want to look at this in a cold-hearted fashion, if you want another reason to pay regularly and on time (other than just living up to the fact you've made a commitment and are therefore honor bound and legally bound), then there's plenty of reason to be found. If and when you skip or are late making these payments, someone other than your ex-wife will surely know. And that may be your children. Now how does that make you feel as a man of integrity? Also, it will inevitably come out in front of your kids that you're a deadbeat dad.

There was a time when I was the co-founder of a start up company, and man, we were really struggling. I mean, really struggling to keep the doors open. We were struggling to make payroll much less pay our vendors. I went a long time without drawing a paycheck. I never went to a judge to try to lower my child support payments, even though my income was less than $1/1000^{th}$ of what it was when I signed the divorce decree – literally less than $1/1000^{th}$! Business associates and friends encouraged me to do this, but I didn't feel it was right, as my ex-wife was not the one who put me in this financial dilemma. This was clearly not her problem.

You know, this sort of reminds me of that line from "Fiddler on the Roof" where the beggar is asking for money. The passer-by explains that times are hard, and he has nothing to give. The beggar comes back with a line that is something like, "Just because you are having a bad week, does that mean that I should have a bad week, too?"

I can say that during that year long period of commercial hell I was late on a few occasions. I always alerted my ex-wife to those tardy payments so she could manage her budget. I'm sure during that time of financial hardship she struggled along with me. But I never, ever missed a payment, as that was the promise I had made to my children through the courts.

I also know that with each of those tardy payments my ex- mother-in-law was probably told of the delays. Now it may occur to you that you don't really care what your ex-mother-in-law thinks of you as a man. But rest assured, whatever she thinks will be shared with your children in some form or fashion – even if it is only by attitude. Who can blame the ex-in-laws? My mom, hell – my entire family, they're very protective and defensive of me. My ex-wife's family is of her and maybe that's as it should be.

Don't screw up your kids by being a deadbeat dad. They are already going to question lots of what happened and where you stand in the "blame-game". Don't give them a reason to wonder or ammunition for someone to convince them that old dad doesn't love them enough to make his monthly payments.

Divorced Dads' Rule #14:
**BE THE PARENT IN YOUR HOME, AND
ENCOURAGE YOUR KIDS' MOM TO BE THE
PARENT IN HER HOME.**

I remember on more than one occasion getting an early morning call that went something like this: "Patrick, I can't get your son up for school."

Now all of a sudden he was *my* son. What a way to start your day! I'm enjoying a nice cup of coffee and the morning sports section, and I get interrupted because I need to be the heavy in somebody else's house. That conversation starter would typically be followed with me saying something like, "all right, put him on the phone…Hey bud, what's going on this morning?"

"I don't want to go to school today, dad," would be the reply.

"Well bud, today's a school day, and you're a school student. So you need to get up, and you need to put on your school shoes, and you need to go to school," would be my next statement.

"Okay," was almost always the response.

In all fairness, it was not an every day or every week occurrence. More like three or four times a year. But after a few years of this, I finally had the impetus to tell my kiddos' mom I was done being the heavy in her house. I told her it was my job to be the dad, but not my job to be the parent in her home. It was unfair for me to be pulled in to negative situations I hadn't helped create and then be expected to resolve them. It was enough for me to take care of my kiddos in my home, and she needed to wear her parent shoes in her home. Now the calls didn't stop completely, but in all honesty, they became less frequent.

Divorced Dads' Rule #15:
GIVE THEM THE BIG HEAD.

It's my contention that the vast majority of the important work as parents is done by the time the kids reach between ages seven and nine.

This is where the foundation is laid. I believe the best we can do is instill love, a social interest, and if possible, the ability to communicate. Those are the gifts we can give our children.

Self-love is of utmost importance. When I look back on all the "sins" I've committed against myself and against others, it's easy for me to see those transgressions are born from a lack of unconditional self-love. This lack of unconditional self-love triggers fear. Fear, F-E-A-R, I believe, is the worst of all four letter words. It drives the unconscious to act out in defense of itself, and we can deliver the most reprehensible of behavior.

Think back to high school, or look to your co-workers, or hell, look in the mirror, and you will see how damaging a lack of unconditional self-love can be. The girls in high school who partied with the football team or were known to be found in the back of any willing boy's car – they were dealing with low self-esteem…. that lack of unconditional self-love. They were looking for attention or acceptance in whatever means they could find it. Trouble was their unconscious actions were self-damning and caused to only increase the feelings of low self-esteem…. that lack of self love. This caused those damning actions to only continue.

Talk about a perpetual motion machine.

Look back to the boys in high school with low self-esteem. These were the yahoos who were acting out their issues in typical aggressive, boorish male behavior. They were the jerks who were continually bullying other boys or the ones getting it on in the back of the cars with the aforementioned girls. Yes, they were the ones telling everybody about it afterwards. They were perpetuating their lack of self-love through violent or misogynistic behavior aimed at other people.

Perhaps you were one of those jerks. Whether you were or weren't – it doesn't really matter now. For it doesn't matter where you've been, it only matters where you are today and where you are going.

If you indeed were one of those bullies, then think back to those days and ask yourself if you truly want your daughter to be that girl in the back seat or that girl running a train with the football team or if you want your son to be that kind of boy. I assume not! Or you wouldn't be reading now.

So the way to help your kiddos not become that low self-esteem high schooler is to constantly feed their own self-esteem and self-love. All kids really need to know is that they are loved, and that there's a safe place for them. I can recall, after the millionth time of reinforcing my kiddos' self-esteem, my ex-wife asking, "Aren't you at all concerned they will grow up to be cocky and total jerks?"

"Hey look," I'd reply. "The world will do what it can to beat them down. They will have as many or more failures as successes in their lives. The fearful people on the planet will go to excruciating length to remind them they've failed or might fail. I want'em armed. I want'em armed with as much ammo for this fight as I can possibly give them. I believe it will be far easier to tame them down later in life than to try to build them up if they don't have a crazy strong foundation. Although, I doubt that'll be necessary as we all pretty much end up scarred and doubtful of ourselves anyway."

So I say, go ahead! Give'em the big head! Make them proud of their every action! Life and the world will keep them in check as times goes by.

Social interest is important for these kids as they're going to live in society. To grow up without empathy and compassion for others makes for a very stilted existence. Teach them about empathy and compassion for others, and couple with that teaching a healthy dose of discernment. To my mind, the best way to get this message across to your children is to simply lead by example. Show them the way to care for and about their fellow man and about the planet in general.

I can remember when Hurricane Katrina knocked New Orleans into the last century. My kiddos and my lady loaded up in our SUV, and we went out and bought every diaper on the shelves from two or three stores. We filled up that SUV, and we drove over to the Star of Hope Mission to unload. We made a game out of it, tossing those diapers to one another and slam-dunking them into the shopping cart. There was nothing serious, and no talks of lessons learned about helping the less fortunate. But I can recall, like it was yesterday, what my son said as we drove off from the Star of Hope's parking lot. And remember, this is coming from a very quiet boy.

"That felt good," that's all he said. But there was a world spoken in those words.

Teach them by example how to treat others. Believe me. They are watching – all of the time.

When I talk about how important the ability to communicate is, what I really mean is to be able to communicate the drivers behind their actions. This is called conscious living – being able to hold up a mirror to themselves and to recognize why they are doing or acting in such a way to some given set of stimuli. Then, teach them to have the ability, once recognized, to communicate that conscious recognition.

Divorced Dads' Rule #16:
DON'T SAY "NO" WHEN YOU CAN SAY "YES".

Life is full of logistical challenges. Life is full of mundane tasks. As a parent, I can tell you, and I can find hundreds of other parents to back this up, that we probably say "no" far too often. If I had one thing to do over again – okay, I probably would have avoided that potato salad at the family picnic back in August of 2000 – but, anyway, for sure, I would have said "no" far less often.

My kids were wee ones and kicking around the house. I was in the kitchen working on our family dinner. My boy comes in, and he wants to throw the ball around outside.

"No," I said, "dad's making dinner."

WHY?

Why does dinner need to be done right then and there? How was our life, how was his life going to be enriched by eating that meal in the next 20 minutes? How much more would his life have been enriched by throwing the ball around for a bit before dinner?

In looking back on my youth, we always ate dinner at the dinner table, and I have great memories of that. But I really cherish those memories of throwing the ball around with my dad and my brothers. Why say "no" when a "no" doesn't make a positive difference and a "yes" does?

This Divorced Dads' Rule falls into the category of being ever present when with your children, a pretty good practice for all other relationships as well.

Divorced Dads' Rule #17:
INCORPORATE THE "RULE OF 3'S" INTO YOUR LIFE.

I have a friendship with a man of high integrity. His name is Brian Adams. No – not that Brian Adams. My buddy, as best I can tell, can't carry a tune in a bucket. I've always referred to him as BA. We met 15 or more years ago. He's a few years younger than me, but in some ways a lifetime ahead of me. BA first explained the "Rule of 3's", and I give him all of the credit. He has since claimed he heard it long before, and it's not originally his. I don't care. Just adopt the "Rule of 3's" into your life, and you will have a better life. And your kids will be all the better for it.

At this point, I'm tempted to give you BA's phone number so you can call him and say thanks. He'd hate that! As I said, I've known BA for many, many years. I know him well enough to know he would say, "Hey, I don't want any credit. Just send checks."

So with that I say, "BA, thanks for the freebie!"

Here is pretty much the "Rule of 3's".

When a dynamic exists in your life, when some issues are raised, when someone cuts you off in traffic, when your boss or a customer is rough on you, when your lady is giving you hell, when a loved one dies (you get the picture), simply apply the "Rule of 3's".

Ask yourself, "How long is this event going to affect my life? Is this going to affect my life for 3 seconds? Is this going to affect my life for 3 minutes? Is this going to affect my life for 3 hours? 3 days? 3 weeks? 3 months? 3 years? Is this going to affect my life for 33 years?"

After you have the answer, simply apply the appropriate amount of energy.

I can tell you this is a wonderful, almost Zen-like approach to living life. It is *almost* living the "sound of one hand clapping" – that release of attachment to the outcome. But it is also harder than hell to live by all of the time. When I recall it in moments of stress, it is of great benefit. I would advise you to consider adopting the "Rule of 3's", and I would advise you to pass it along to your children.

My children know the "Rule of 3's".

Divorced Dads' Rule #18:
GO BUY A FLOWERED APRON.

So, up to now, you've been the kids' dad. Now that you're a divorced dad, you take on an additional role. At times in your home, you must also fill the role of mom.

Nothing has touched me quite like getting Mother's Day cards from my sisters to honor the maternal aspect of my parenting. Now this may seem like an uncomfortable pair of shoes to wear. Hey, at least you don't have to put on the high heels! Although, that's your option!

As I said, it is necessary at times to fill the role of mom. I mean, just try to not be the matriarch of your family when your little child falls off her bike for the first time. Never mind that it's only 1 ½ minutes into that ride! You can't do it. You have a nurturing side to you, and they need to see it come out. Hell! They need that compassion at times. When the kids are with you, it will be necessary to do motherly things. And it will come more naturally than you could ever expect.

First off, go stock the medicine cabinet. Look, men typically have very little stuff in their cabinet, and kids need kid-meds. You can simply go to the pharmacist at your local drugstore, and tell them what you're trying to get accomplished. You'd be surprised how much crap you have to buy to keep a well-stocked med cabinet to address the maladies of children – from child thermometers, to non-rancid tasting cough meds, to Benadryl – and man the list goes on. There's a ton of information on the internet – go figure, huh? And most of it comes from pretty good sources.

And for God's sake, don't forget to get those fun cartoon band-aids. They will make all the boo-boos heal faster.

Cook meals, real meals – not just taking the stuff out of the box and tossing it into the microwave. There's nothing like sitting at the dinner table with your children and eating a real, healthy, home-cooked meal which you've prepared. Your wife isn't around to do it, if she ever did, so you might as well step up to the stove. Rustle up some vittles. It's not as daunting as it first seems. Hell, there's a ton of great male chefs in this world! Cooking stuff on the stove is not all that different than grilling meats and vegetables on the grill. The cookbooks are really written – well…kind of like cookbooks, if you will. All you have to do is follow the directions. There are a ton of 15 minute recipe books at the bookstore, and they don't necessarily require a microwave.

And don't feel intimated. Your mom had to learn at some point, your ex-wife had to learn at some point, and she isn't all that smart! After all, she married you, didn't she?

While you're at it, go ahead and get all the kitchen stuff: nice plates, silverware, glasses, serving bowls, etc. Integrate the kids into the process. Get them to help you cook and clean up. They get a kick out of setting the table, and older kids actually appreciate that you took the time to prepare a meal. They may even enjoy cooking with you. For goodness sakes, at least take the Chinese out of the to-go boxes, and put the food on a serving plate. Seriously, kids actually appreciate this kind of stuff.

Now, you don't have to go all "Martha-Stewart" on this, but presentation is about 80% of the deal. That is unless you have a kid like my son. He was about nine years old when he uttered the following words, "Dad, no offense or anything, but this white sauce tastes like ass." This was after I had painstakingly served up an intricately prepared five-course meal. This was a big Sunday dinner.

"No offense taken," was all I could think of (the little jerk!). I was hiding my smile the entire time, and also biting my tongue from the want to continue, "Look, you little rat, you've never made homemade hollandaise sauce. It took forever." But what are you going to do? It probably did taste bad to him.

Another story about playing the role of mom, again new shoes for dad, comes to mind when I think of returning to school and buying school clothes for the kiddos. I felt like this was important as it was about our home being a home, not turning those motherly tasks over to mom. It has been my experience that every dynamic has heightened drama for preteen girls. Just allow her to have that energy, and try not to catch those energy-field balls when she throws them at you.

So my daughter was beginning junior high school and came to me to discuss a serious dilemma. "Dad, you know that in junior high we dress for PE and everything together, right?"

"Ya, so what?"

"Well dad, I need some new panties. I mean, I can't wear my Barney panties in the locker room without getting embarrassed. I mean, they're real comfortable and everything, but I need some new ones."

Wow, it had never dawned on me. Here was a kid who had only grown taller in the past handful of years and hadn't started to round out physically. She was very long but rail thin. The underwear I had bought for her all those years ago still fit. Now that she raised the issue, I realized we hadn't ever replaced her childhood undergarments. No wonder those Barney panties were comfortable. Is there anything as comfortable as threadbare, years-old drawers? Man, was I asleep at the job! A trip to the mall cleared away any and all negligence on this one.

Continuing on with the motherly manner of being a divorced dad: Do those little things that make memories – plants in the house, hang their artwork up on the fridge, hang their artwork and photos in the den, bedrooms…. everywhere.

Divorced Dads' Rule #19:
BE A HOMEROOM DAD.

Believe me – the teachers will treat your kids better if they think ol' divorced dad is taking good care of the kids.

There have been plenty of studies on caregivers' treatment of senior citizens in those old folks' homes. The residents who got frequent visitors were more humanized; and therefore, they are treated better by the staff. Teachers, I have found, can succumb to similar influences.

Go to the school, and do stuff. You can volunteer for PTA and PTO if you've got the stamina. I surely didn't. You can, however, show up at school once a week or once a month and read to the kids' classes. You'll get to know the teachers and the classmates, and it will give you some context to your kids' conversations about school. It may also give the teacher one more reason to like your kid, and that is priceless.

Now, I'd go to both my kids' classes to read once a month. Every time I went, I would take a Shel Silverstein book with me. He's got great poems that are silly, nonsensical, and poke fun at life. You know, all the stuff little kids like. I also, without fail, read "Jabberwocky" by Lewis Carroll. Now this poem, I read with an outlandish pirate accent, and the kids got into it in ways I would never have imagined. I'd tell the front row, just before I launched into my Blackbeard's version of "Jabberwocky", "Clear out guys, you've got to move back, because I'm probably going to spit when I read this thing." The little ones loved this outlandish and quite frankly, childish behavior. And quite frankly so did I.

After reading "J-Wocky" to my daughter's class for about six months in a row, my daughter asked me not to bring it with me on my next reading session. Now the kids requested "Jabberwocky" when I finished reading the Shel Silverstein poems, and I told them I didn't bring the book this time because my daughter asked me not to bring it. Then I told them I had one last poem for them. I opened the Silverstein book, and I looked right in my daughter's eyes and launched into, with all my pirate's glory, "*'Twas brillig, and the slithy toves...*" from "Jabberwocky". Laughingly, I pointed at my daughter, and I said, "You told me not to bring the book, but you didn't tell me not to memorize the poem."

The kids thought this was a hysterical moment, and then they all chimed in to complete the poem, as they'd memorized it over the last few months. This was a fun memory for those kids, and frankly a proud moment of good parenting on my part. For even though she wouldn't admit it at the time, my daughter was proud I was her daddy. I could see it in her eyes. Be silly with little kids. Let your guard down, and be silly. Do it often.

Now the positive outcome of me showing up at school was that my kids kind of got special treatment from some of the teachers and counselors. I'll take my time away from work as a great investment for that return any day of the week.

Divorced Dads' Rule #20:
BE THE COACH.

Coach anything, coach everything.

Get involved somehow in the dance or sports programs or whatever your daughter or son is interested in. If you don't have time to do the team coach thing, then volunteer to be assistant or scorekeeper or team mom. Hey – dads can bring cupcakes too. Just being around the kids at these functions makes memories for them. Just the time in the car can make for valuable parenting. You have, after all, a captive audience in that moment. It also forces you to spend more time with your kids and their friends.

However, as important as anything else, being around these situations makes certain that any inappropriate adult behavior toward your kids or their friends is witnessed and managed by you. There's a very high probability your kid is going to experience behavior directed toward them from some backstage mom or tough love baseball coach. Adults far too often are trying to fulfill their unrealized dreams in these situations, and they will surely project a ton of negative energy towards your kid.

Be there to guard them against this behavior.

Speaking of coaching, here's a tip that may make a difference if you can keep it in mind. Whenever I coached my kids in a sport, I always made this promise to them prior to the start of the season.

"Guys, when I'm out there coaching, I don't want the other team or the other coaches or the other parents to know you're my kid. I don't want to treat you any better or any worse than I treat all the other kids," then I would add with an evil laugh, "at least not while we're at the games!"

Now, this was a promise I made to my guys, and a promise I made to myself. I thought it would keep me from projecting too much of my stuff onto my children. I didn't want to be one of those jerk dads who yelled at their kids whenever they dropped a ball or blew a pass on a fast break. Those guys should be gut-shot as far as I'm concerned.

Remember always the words of Karl Gustav Jung, and I paraphrase here: "Parental projection is the worst sin that parents can commit against their children". Avoid projection at all costs. You can't do this, you can't completely do this, but you should try at all times.

My son was doing the Cub Scout thing, and man, I hated this stuff. I'd never done the scouts as a kid, and I saw the meetings as very boring. All it seemed we ever did was say the "Pledge of Allegiance" then sit there for an hour while kid after kid paraded up to get his merit badge for underwater basket weaving or whatever. The annual Cub Scout cake bake-off and auction came around, and it was finally time we got a badge. It just so happened the cake auction occurred on the evening of an out-of-town business trip. I figured out the logistics, and I knew that if I baked the cake the night before, and I put it in my SUV with all the cake-decorating frosting and all the stuff, that we'd have about an hour or so to get it done. I pegged the maximum-minimum drive time from my meeting in Austin to Houston, and I figured I had a drop-dead departure time of 3:00 pm. I explained at the onset of my meeting with my prospective customer that I had to be out by 3:00 pm, and all seemed okay.

I rolled into my ex-wife's house to decorate the cake with my little Cub Scout, and I asked him what he wanted to make. We had an hour to burn.

"A jack-o-lantern," was his response, "with worms coming out of his eyes!"

"Okay – you're on man. I'll mix up some orange icing." And I began. He went to town on that round cake and orange icing, and it actually looked pretty cool. By the time he put the black outline on the mouth and eyes, we kind of had a gray-black gooey smudge of a cake with hints of orange poking out from behind this cloudy haze. And he did indeed top it off with gummy worms crawling out of that jack-o-lantern's smudged eyes. This thing looked like hell. Better yet, it looked like a reject from hell.

At this point my ex-wife took me aside and said, "Look, you don't know what a big deal this thing is. There'll be frickin' Eiffel Tower cakes, built to scale no less. He's going to be humiliated."

I nodded, and then I asked my son, "Hey bud, whatcha think of your cake?"

"I'll probably win," he flatly replied.

I winked at his mom, looked at him, looked at the cake, and announced, "Let's roll!"

Wow, she was right. And yes, there even was an Eiffel Tower cake. And it did appear to be built to scale. The most impressive of all 50 cakes was this black widow spider cake. Maybe I failed to mention this event happened around Halloween. The spider was huge, and it had a web of spun chocolate. Martha Stewart would have been green with envy.

Now the notion of this auction was that no cake would go for more than $10, and every cake would be bought. In case of tying $10 bids, they would dispense numbers and a lottery would ensue. We put $10 down on that spider cake, which was my son's choice. We took our number as everybody bid on that damn cake. It was an awesome looking piece of art! I also intended to give someone a ten spot to bid on our cake, just to make sure it got picked up. This wasn't necessary, as while we were standing over the table with our cake, a lady walked up and asked, "Who did this jack-o-lantern?"

My boy shot back, "That one's mine! We'll probably win something." She looked at me and smiled and put down her $10 on that damn smudged-up cake.

God bless that woman, whoever she was.

Well, we won the bid on the spider cake, and the lady went home with the orange smudge cake. We went back to his mom's house after the affair, toting the spider cake with its fancy frosting web. His mom made a huge deal over the intricacy of that spider cake, and she asked how the evening had gone.

To which my son replied, "It was great!"

I then told her about all the other cakes, and how none of them fetched more at auction than our boy's cake. Now, remember they all topped out at $10 even. I finally asked my son how much time he thought those kids put into all their fancy cakes.

He looked me square in the eyes and said, "Probably not any time, dad. Their moms and dads probably did it all while they watched TV."

Out of the mouths of babes, huh?

That spider cake ate no better or worse than that circular, smudged-up jack-o-lantern confection that some kind woman had taken home to her assumedly chagrined family.

And, lest I forget, while you're shopping for that flowered apron, get an iron. Nothing says divorced dad, or kids from a broken home like wrinkled clothes. Seriously, this one's a dead giveaway. Also, watch out for bed-head at school, huh? The teachers will definitely peg your kids as divorce kids if they bail out of dad's car with crazy "Flock of Seagulls" bed-head. There's an easy fix to this. Just buy some of that "Bed-Head" spray and wet down their heads before school. Believe me – the teachers will treat your kid better if they think dad is taking good care of them.

When my son was a wee one, he had some kind of trouble getting prepped for school. His morning motor ran at glacial speed. Hell, who am I kidding? He still has trouble – fifteen years old, 6'2", 230 lbs – mornings are still tough for that boy. He was in 1st grade – and not in a place where he focused so well on the objective at hand. Getting ready for school in the morning was a struggle for this little guy. First, there are all the steps to that process, and second was the fact that this occurred in the morning and he was a sleepy head.

On school days this was cause for inordinate struggle and persistent yelling at his mom's house. I wasn't going to go that route, and I came up with an alternative plan for our house. I would place his homework, his shoes, his socks, his shorts, t-shirt, his breakfast and lunch in the car in the morning before I woke him. All he had to do in those mornings was brush his teeth and get his butt in the car. And I was flexible on the teeth brushing. After all, they really are just practice teeth. They're going to fall out regardless of brushing! (Okay, go ahead, alert CPS about my parenting style, but we made it through all of that and they both have nice smiles.)

A friend once asked me, "Aren't you worried about enabling him by taking care of all his needs?"

A fair question I thought. Then I said, "Hey look. All I want to do is get outta' the house without any yelling. Hell, if I tell that kid to go upstairs and get his shoes and socks, I'm liable to find him two minutes later upstairs playing with his toy cars."

This plan did indeed work. And over time, he was able to take care of himself.

Divorced Dads' Rule #21:
ACCEPT THAT YOU AND YOUR EX- WILL PARENT DIFFERENTLY.

A recently divorced buddy of mine, who has a young child, made the following comment, and it made good sense. Thanks to you, Daniel, for contributing to other divorced dads!

We were talking on the subject of dealing with the different parenting styles from one house to the other – mom's house rules versus dad's house rules. I told him this was often a part of the glass-eating we divorced dads must do and surely it's the same for divorced moms. He replied, "You know, Patrick, I kind of look at it like when the kids go over to the grandparents' house. You can tell them you don't want the kids eating junk, and you don't want the kids staying up past their bedtime; but once you drive off, the grandparents are going to do whatever they want to do."

I feel he has a good perspective, but it must be considered conditionally. Some of the tension around the subject is surely about control issues, and some of this tension is surely about feeling that nobody can care for your child better than you can. And some of this tension is about simply disagreeing with one another's parenting styles and choices.

The feeling of need to control, to some degree, must be released, as you are not present at all times. By the way, recognizing this need to control is all borne of fear may help. Just accept that your ex- is going to have different opinions, attitudes, and approaches to parenting. She will surely have to accept the same of you.

In matters that are significant, you must assert yourself. I can remember one time going over to my parents' home, and their car was gone. They were gone, and our two kids were gone. On letting myself into their home, I saw the two kids' car seats were sitting in the den. A short time later, my parents rolled up in the car with the kiddos in the back, obviously not in car seats. My parents and I had a conversation unlike any before or since. It was the first time I actually admonished my parents. I told them the kiddos were entrusted into their care, and while rules at grandma's and grandpa's house were no doubt different, some rules like safety and car seats must be consistent. I went on to tell them that future violations of these sacred rules would mean we couldn't leave the kids alone with them.

It was weird talking to my parents like that. It was like some role-swapping scene from "Parent Trap" or something, but they understood I was resolute. And they accepted my terms. In all fairness to them, they raised eight kids without car seats, and they had just driven two blocks to my aunt's house. Putting those kids in their car seats for a two block drive, knowing the seats would have to be removed upon return, just didn't make sense to them. It would have taken longer to put in and then pull out those two car seats (man, they are such a pain!) than to make the drive itself. There's no traffic on the streets of their old neighborhood. Perhaps in retrospect, I was being too stern, but at the time I felt some rules were too important to break. I also went back to that thought of, "how would I feel if a tragedy occurred just because I was cutting corners to save five minutes?"

My kids' mom has a distinctly different parenting style than mine. Upon casual observation, one might believe she was stricter with our kiddos than me. She was quick to jump on them, and she raised her voice frequently. I, on the other hand, came across as laid back and seemingly very accepting of most behavior. But the difference in our style was that while she was quick to jump on them, her bark was far worse than her bite. I would allow loose behavior, but at the point where unacceptable behavior was encountered, I would hold firm on my convictions. The kids knew at my house I would seldom raise my voice. But when I said, "You're about to cross the line of acceptable behavior," they knew repercussions would follow. I believe that conversely, they knew at mom's house she would raise her voice, but that she would infrequently follow through with firm consequences.

Kids are very adaptable. They can figure out in little time what is acceptable in one house and unacceptable in the other. No need to compromise your parenting beliefs to meet some middle ground to make things easier for the kids on the house switch. Stick to your guns, and they will figure it out in your home. Sometimes a reminder of what house they are in is all that is necessary. Remember to be consistent in your house, by all means. Be consistent.

There's another story that reminds me of a better way to handle the differences you may have with your ex-wife in this whole child rearing arena. This story is told with far more calm and humor than when the event actually occurred. I was at my nephew's high school football game sitting next to my sister, my great child rearing mentor. My junior high school-age daughter was sitting directly in front of me and leaned forward as she talked with her cousin. Out from under my baby girl's blue jeans popped a superman emblem attached to the tiniest red thong I had ever seen. Man, this locked me up. I almost spit out my nachos. My sister leaned over, and she said, "Can you believe that shit?"

"Look, I'm trying not to go off right now, but we'll figure this one out soon enough!" I said.

I never mentioned this episode to my daughter or to my ex-wife, but as I recall, that thong, and all subsequent "fatherly-deemed inappropriate attire", was a casualty to the washer and dryer experience. It seems those thongs somehow never made it from the washer to the dryer when we were doing clothes at my house. Point to that story, there are multiple ways of handling the situation. My personality, historically, has been one of confrontation. Take the issue head on. In this case, I ruffled no feathers and dealt with the issue in a passive manner, but I resolved the issue in my home.

Another passive-aggressive approach came during a conversation with my daughter, still in those junior high years. "Dad," she coaxed, "mom doesn't want me to get the cartilage in my ears pierced. Can you take me?"

I took a page from my father, who sat silently at dinner one night back in the 70s as my older brother rolled into the house with an earring. Dad never said a word. His silence took all the shock value away. I remember my brother being somewhat deflated, deflated that his new accoutrement would elicit no response from the old man.

In a very matter of fact manner, I told my daughter, "Nope, I don't want you to get your cartilage pierced so I won't take you. And I surely don't want to do something in defiance of your mom's wishes." This seemed like a ripe opportunity to deliver the message that I was, as often as possible, going to at least attempt to co-parent with her mom. "But, if you want to get your eyebrow or bellybutton, or lips pierced, or even a Monroe, we can do that," I continued on.

"What? I don't want any of that stuff. I just want to get another earring in my ear," she said.

I went on, "Hey look, if I'm not okay with the cartilage piercing, but I'm okay with the other stuff, at least you can't say I'm not cool. Only a cool dad would allow that stuff."

She knew in that moment I had judo-moved her argument away from her before she even had a chance to raise the issue.

Now, I would have never gone in that direction if I had thought for a moment she would have taken me up on the other stuff. She wasn't that radical with the whole piercing thing. And I knew she wouldn't take me up on the other options. If she would have called my bluff, I'd have been hosed.

Divorced Dads' Rule #22:
**WHEN WITH YOUR CHILDREN, SAVE ENOUGH
ENERGY TO BE IN THE MOMENT.**

Hey, take a note from the book of the Zen masters; and when with your children, always be present.

Be in the moment.

How many times have parents looked back on child rearing moments and realized they were elsewhere when their kids needed them? These moments will sneak up on you, and then they're gone. Lost is the opportunity to make a difference in that particular moment – that moment in your child's time of need. These moments come at the most random of times.

It can be as simple as a situation of you making dinner in the kitchen, and your kid comes in to ask for something. "Maybe later, not right now, dad's cooking dinner," we might say. These are lousy responses to little kids. They don't get what "later" means. All they know is they felt a need, and it went unmet by their parent.

I'd love to have all those times back when my son walked up to me and said, "Dad, can we go throw the ball?"

Those times I responded, "Not now bud, I'm in the middle of _____ (fill in the blank)."

This is not to say he didn't wear my arm out throwing footballs and baseballs. In retrospect, even one time of saying "no" is one too many.

Look – dinner can wait, the bills can wait, washing the clothes can wait, cleaning the garage can wait. Folks will tell you if you do what I say, then you don't teach them about patience. They'll tell you kids need to learn delayed gratification. It's a childhood lesson they'll say. They'll tell you all these things. I tell you they are wrong!

Don't worry about spoiling them when they're little. The world's going to put them in situations time and time again as they mature, and they'll come to learn about patience and delayed gratification. In your home, be there for them. Look – we're not going to go to our death beds looking back on time spent on those mundane tasks.

We'll surely go to our death beds looking back on fun times shared with those we love.

Be there for them.

It may take some adapting to apply this, but practicing being in the present will curb many negative responses. This may serve you well in other relationships.

Not being in the present will also cause other negative behavior or reaction to your kids' actions.

Now, one of the stories that speaks to this is probably more deeply etched into my mind than it is into my son's memory bank. For whatever reason, and I believe it's because I can still see that look in his eyes, this one sticks out like a sore thumb.

I walked into the kitchen one morning, and I found my five year old son standing over a very large and very broken bowl of cake mix. I'd been making a cake for his sister's birthday, and I'd left the kitchen for no more than five minutes. Is there anything more tempting to a little one than licking the bowl or spoon of a cake mix? I'm not sure what or how it happened, but he brought that bowl crashing down on the kitchen floor. There I found him standing over it with a look of total surprise on his face.

"Man, how come you always break *everything*?" I asked.

(Okay, okay, so this is not my most proud parenting moment.)

"How come you *always ask me* that question?" he asked, looking up at me with those huge golden eyes of his.

Wow! I felt an inch tall.

Man, this sucked. Because I knew in that moment, I'd left a mark on my boy. I'm certain I had never asked him that question before, and I doubt his mom had either. But in his mind, he believed that to be the case. The truth is the little guy broke stuff all the time. He was a rough and tumble guy, and it always seemed that he, even as a little kid, had the touch of a blacksmith.

114

No doubt about it, you will give your kids reasons to do couch time. As a matter of fact, as mine got older and we would have disagreements on my manner of parenting, I'd often half jokingly say, "Well, when you get older, this may be another conversation for you to bring up with your therapist."

Another comment I would admit to my children when we encountered some parent-child strife was, "Hey guys, this is my first time at this parenting thing just like it is your first time at being a kid. I am trying to do the best I can, and hopefully you can appreciate that we may disagree. But at least we are both putting in effort to be good at this thing."

The reality is this. In retrospect, if I were judged as a parent on my worst moments, then I would probably be in CPS' files. But if judged, as I hope, on my body of work as a parent, then I'll fare pretty well. Reality is, I guess, this could be said of all my relationships.

So, at least for your children, be there for them, be in the moment, at all times. Try to "still the noise". If you can do it with other relationships, then that is all the better.

Your kids will give you ample opportunity to train yourself to become the samurai in this dynamic.

Be that samurai.

Here's a tip. I did not execute well at this one. Kids will ask a lot of questions during the time you're around. When they ask a question, answer the question they ask, and then clam up. Sometimes they want to delve further. Other times the answer to that one question will satisfy them. I've always been one to go on and on and elaborate and make every situation a learning opportunity. If my kids ever write a book about ol' dad, trust me, there will be a chapter or more on how I always went on and on and on. They tease me about it now, and frankly, it's quite funny when I look back.

Just give'em what they ask for. If they want more, they will ask.

Divorced Dads' Rule #23:
READ SOMETHING, ANYTHING, ON A FREQUENT BASIS.

Reading to your kids is a big deal.

I also believe that reading in front of your kids is a huge influence on their cognitive development. Creating a ritual of reading at bedtime can make for some very intimate conversations. They're tired and ready to drift off to dreamland. In those moments, they may let their guards down just enough to ask you some question or questions that have been nagging at them for some time. Their sleepiness disarms them a bit. Be brief in these moments with your answers, as their ability to stay on task at such a time is really minimal.

But it's the questions themselves which may give you a wonderful glimpse into where your kids are emotionally.

Back to reading.

Hopefully you have interest in something. Read books or subscribe to magazines that cater to your interest, whatever it takes to get you reading in front of your kids. Seeing their dad read on a regular basis, hey – this is especially true for the little kids between the ages of 1 and 10, has been proven to open kids' minds to the power and adventure of reading.

(If you don't believe this, I suggest you go to the internet and check it out. After all, if it is on the internet, it has to be true...right?)

If you think it doesn't matter whether or not your kids read, then I suggest you check yourself. Kids who have an appreciation for reading do far better in school. They will have a far more developed vocabulary. And books, books on varied subjects and varied cultures, can also help open the children's minds. Talk to someone who is an avid reader, and you will come away with the realization they, at the very least, have an enhanced vocabulary. And that can make some difference in life.

I don't care if you're a bibliophile or just read trade magazines. I don't care if all you read are fishing magazines. It simply doesn't matter. Just lead by example, and show them the written word has great value.

Take them to the bookstore or the local library. Let them pick out their own books. It's a pretty good plan. It gives them a sense of ownership or pride around that book. And don't harangue them to finish the book they bought or checked out. It's their book, let them read it or not. I assure you that beating them over the head about books is not a recommended plan to get them to love books.

As my guys got older, I found my book recommendations were falling on deaf ears. I mean, as far as they were concerned, what the hell did I know? I realized quite by accident that probably the best way to encourage kids to read is to just leave the books on the coffee table rather than to drum it into their heads how great the book is. Stick a post-it note or whatever to mark the chapter you want them to read. But don't say anything. Chances are they'll at least flip through that marked spot just out of curiosity. They might even give it a read. If they're interested, they'll take it upon themselves to get into that book. But leave it to them.

Again, that notion of release of outcome, release of expectations, nay - the sound of one hand clapping - comes through as a shining parenting principle.

And by all means, if you are a "reader" of men's magazines, keep them where the kids will never find them. The kids don't need to know that ol' dad is one of those men who objectify women, as you are trying to become the man of integrity you want your son to become and the man of integrity you want your daughter to partner with, or hey, your son to partner with. Keep an open mind, huh?

Divorced Dads' Rule #24:
SHUT DOWN THOSE PROJECTORS.

Speaking of projection, it doesn't only come from the parents or grandparents. Projection comes at our kids and at us from every angle.

Here are two stories: one about someone's projection onto my daughter, and the other about someone's projection onto my son.

My daughter's freshman year in high school found her in the homecoming court. I guess some things haven't changed all that much since I was in high school in Texas. But it's my assumption, at least in Texas, the pageantry associated with homecoming and prom has grown as if it were on steroids. As part of being in the homecoming court, my daughter and I were to walk arm-in-arm to mid-field at half time of the big homecoming football game. They would announce our names and all the accomplishments that made her "homecoming court material".

We both got dressed up, as we needed to fit in with the rest of the pageant participants, and out we walked. As we walked along the out-of-bounds line and got to the 50 yard line to make that turn onto midfield, a lady said to my daughter, "Smile honey, this is the biggest day of your life!"

My daughter put on a Hollywood smile for the lady and speaking through her clenched teeth said to me, "Oh God, Dad, I hope this isn't the biggest day of my life! I hope my life holds far more than this."

I laughed, and I told her perhaps it was the biggest day of that lady's life. But I was for sure betting she would have many more outstanding, far more memorable days than this. People will push their stuff onto your kids at every turn, and your job as a parent is to keep those kids on their true path and not the one that you or someone else wants to project onto them. Let them live their lives.

My daughter had all new projection visited on her recently when she graduated from high school. We had a chance to talk about how significant and insignificant high school graduation really is. We talked about it merely being a passage – not unlike many other coming or historic passages in her life. This was simply another change of shoes. I did tell her, however, that one great aspect

123

about this passage was she now had an opportunity to completely reinvent herself if she so chose. I told her she was going off to college and only about 10 out of 40,000 people would have any notion of who she was. She now could become whoever she wanted to be. Heck, I told her she could even put on a British accent if she so chose. Nobody would know any better of it.

The real point to this is she could finally be exactly who she wanted to be – free from the constraints and projections of her mom and dad and teachers and grandparents and others. She could put away any and all masks she may have been wearing in the past and open up that wonderful life she chooses. She could step into her dance shoes and dance. Dance in her true shoes.

The male version of parental projection came no doubt from one of my many, many encounters with little league dads. My son was a hell of an athlete. He now stands 6'2" and 230 lbs as a 15 year old. He played most sports when he was younger, and I coached most of his teams. My reason for coaching was to make sure no little league dads ruined this experience. I had seen enough of that stuff by those backstage moms who infiltrated my daughter's theater experiences.

Well, one baseball game we were getting killed. I mean the other team was run-ruling us on every inning. The 3rd base coach for the opposing team had his kids steal on every pitch, I mean every frickin' pitch they were running! Our catcher was not any good, and the kid was a wreck from the tension of dealing with all those base runners. Kids know when they aren't having a shining moment, just like we do, and they tighten up. This kid was totally locked up.

"Hey bud," I hollered from the dugout to the other coach. "Why don't you take your foot off the gas a bit and quit stealing on every pitch? Give this catcher a break, man. He's freaking out back there."

"You teach your catcher to catch, and I'll teach my kids how to steal," was his curt reply.

I wanted to walk out of that dugout and strangle that jerk right there on the spot. Instead, I walked out the back gate of the dugout and walked around under the bleachers until I calmed down.

I'm from the day when dads brought their coolers to the baseball game and drank Schlitz in a can while their sons played ball. Trust me, as a kid, I'd seen my fair share of little league dads going at it with the umpire or other dads. Fist fighting dads at the ballpark! What a great memory from my childhood! I wasn't about to put those images into my son's or his teammates' heads. Finally, I walked back into the dugout. They were still stealing on us (every pitch!), which by now was almost always passed as our catcher had the yips.

Well, I'd had enough of this crap. I got as close to that 3rd base coach as I could while staying in our dugout and quietly said, "Hey man, just because you got cut from the team when you were a freshman doesn't mean you gotta' take it out on these 10 year old boys."

For some reason the guy stopped sending the runners. I don't know why, and I don't care why. I only care that he backed off the throttle.

Parents get awfully caught up in projecting their stuff onto their kids' lives. Make sure you don't, and make sure you defend the innocent ones when you see it being done to them.

Divorced Dads' Rule #25:
TEACH YOUR CHILDREN ACCEPTANCE AND DIVERSITY.

We've taken an annual pilgrimage to New Orleans Jazz and Heritage Festival every year since my kids were born. These kids have cut their teeth on Dr. John, the Neville Brothers, Irma Thomas and countless others. My daughter is now 17. She's been to 16 Jazz Fests. My son is 15, and he's been there 13 times.

(This is a great festival, but I'm actually not promoting it to you. I don't want to increase the crowds by even one. I'm merely using the story from Jazz Fest to talk about teaching acceptance and diversity.)

One year when my guys were around seven and five years old, a lady walked up to me at Jazz Fest and started asking me questions about bringing kids to the Fest. She had a young daughter, and she wanted to know what it would be like. I told her I'd been to 20 years of Jazz Fest and spent an average of seven days per year reveling in the magic. I then said I didn't know but that I estimated about 50,000 people attended per Fest day. That must be something over 5 million people who've shared the Fest with me over all those years, and I've never once seen a fight or any altercation whatsoever. So I told her I thought the Fest was quite safe for kids.

I then went on – as you can tell I'm never one short with words – to tell her to take a look at the guy rolling on the ground with my little kids. That kid had come over earlier and asked if he could rumble with my children. He explained he was from California, and he was in New Orleans for college, and he missed his two brothers and sisters who were about my kids' ages.

I told her, "You see that kid over there having a squirt gun fight with my kids? Well, I don't know him. I've never seen him before, and I'll probably never see him again."

The college kid was on the ground trying to wrestle a squirt gun away from my son, while my daughter soaked him with hers. He was a shaved-headed, pierced-eared, soul patch wearing, no shirt, two-tattoo sporting, blue jean cutoff wearing, no shoes kid wrestler.

I told her my kids spent half their lives in suburbia with their mom and half their lives in town with me. I also said that to them this kid was normal because they had been exposed to this type of person over the years at Jazz Fest and other adventures with ol' dad. But if that kid were to walk down the street in their white-bred suburban area, somebody would no doubt call the cops.

My kids have grown up not fully understanding racism, other than the fact that some people have some real mucked up issues with intolerances and differences.

Speaking of racism, I'm reminded of a story with my kiddos.

Every Monday I used to drive from Houston to Austin for the day, and I'd typically listen to books on tapes during the drive. One day we were in the car, and I was hopping out to get some ice and drinks at the convenience store.

"Ya'll wanna come in?" I asked as I popped open the door.

"Actually dad, I'd like to stay in the car and listen to this girl talk. I'm trying to get her accent down," was my daughter's reply.

The tape in the player at the time was "To Kill a Mockingbird" by Harper Lee, and the story was told in the voice of a young, southern female.

When I returned from the store, I fired up the car.

"Dad, what's a nigger?" was the question from the back seat.

I hadn't realized the story was at the courtroom scene in the book. Wow, I thought. How good is my life? I have a nine year old daughter and a seven year old son, and they don't know the meaning of the word "nigger".

To fully appreciate this you must realize I was born in the early '60s in a very blue collar area of southeast Houston. That word was part of my early years on a daily basis. Nobody ever thought twice about denigrating another with that term – black or white. Now, here we were, and my kids didn't even know what it meant.

Perhaps we're making progress in this world after all.

"Well guys, 'nigger' is a word people used to use, and some still do, to talk badly about other people. It's not a nice word at all. It's used as a bad word often times in references to black-skinned people. You see, some people are scared of differences in other people, and some people take that fear, and they turn it into hatred for people who are different from them. As a matter of fact, everybody is different from everybody else. And it's not only black people that have dealt with being treated badly by others. As a matter of fact, you guys have Irish blood in your veins because your great-grandparents are from Ireland. And at one time the Irish people in the United States were treated as lowest of the low. People treated them like they were less than human. Some folks just can't get beyond their fears of people who are different, and they treat them really bad. They call that being *prejudiced* against someone or some group of people like Irish people or black people or even people from different religions. And since we are all different from each other, pretty much everybody has had their turn at being treated badly by these scared, prejudiced types of people," I explained.

I went on to further explain that this prejudice can even happen when people from different colored skins or different religions got married. Some people thought that was wrong.

Now, I must interject into this story that my younger brother, Andrew, is married to a woman from Trinidad. He met her years ago on a surfing adventure down there, as he's quite the surfer. He spends a lot of time out in the sun chasing those tasty waves.

"Hey, that's not fair," my son declared from the back seat as we drove off, "that's like saying that a short person can't marry a tall person or a fat person can't marry a skinny person."

"Exactly!" I exclaimed, recognizing he got it.

"I mean that's like saying a blonde haired person can't marry a black haired person," he went on.

"Exactly!" I exclaimed.

"I mean, Dad! That's like Uncle Andy and Aunt Alicia!" he went on incredulously.

"Exactly!" I chimed in.

"I mean, Uncle Andy is black-skinned, and Aunt Alicia is white skinned," he concluded.

"Exactly!" I concurred without missing a beat.

Wow! Was I going to love telling my "black-skinned", Caucasian brother that story! I called him an hour later, but his Trini wife answered. He was out. I told her the story, and she just laughed and laughed, and said, "Ya know, boyee! I tell 'dat brudder of yours all 'de time 'dat he more Trini 'dan me!"

Perhaps…perhaps… perhaps, we are making progress.

I have heard from my kids over the years how weak some people are when they express prejudice against others over race or religion or sexual preference.

Perhaps….

Divorced Dads' Rule #26:
MAKE LASTING MEMORIES.

Kids pretty quickly grow out of the need for lots of this behavior from you. I can recall when my son was in 5th grade. I appeared at his school with a cake and one of those huge birthday cookies. Ol' dad thought this would go over well for the birthday boy at his lunchtime. Well, as I walked into the cafeteria, I could see some of his buddies were getting pumped up about getting cake and cookies. My son had different thoughts. He walked over to me, and he quietly said, "Hey dad, thanks a lot and everything, but you can stop doing this stuff now."

I said, "Hey, gotcha bud. From now on, we'll not celebrate your birthday at school – only at home. Next year, I'm going to leave you alone at school lunch."

He looked up relieved and said, "Thanks dad. But, could we start right now? I mean, can you take this stuff home? I'm embarrassed."

Once again, when you look them in the eye and you've drummed honesty in their heads from the start, you can't argue with that. So we ate the stuff at the house, and I never interrupted his school lunch again.

Take them to museums, take them to the fair, and take them to the zoo and to parades. Take'em everywhere. Make memories.

Take them everywhere. An example from our lives is that every summer we would rent the same old beat up beach house. The kids loved it, and it made for an annual pilgrimage. We also, every New Year's (and I tried to get the woman I was dating to buy off on this one) make crazy hats and put them on and dance around the house at midnight. Okay, the reality is that I would typically set the clock ahead about two hours, and we'd have our midnight in Houston about an hour before the ball would drop in New York. Then the kiddos were off to bed, and I was off to have champagne with my lady. Of course, this stuff only works when the kids are little. Teens typically don't want to hang out with the parents on New Year's. Enjoy this stuff when they are young because then you have more control over what they do on New Year's and other celebrations. Be silly with them, and make a ton of memories.

It's not that difficult to muster up the energy to do all these things - you're making memories for these guys, and you're making memories for yourself. They soak up all of this stuff like sponges, and end up with a zest for trying new adventures in life. Take them everywhere. I'll always contend that I'd forgotten how to climb a tree until I became a dad. And now I vow to climb a tree every year. My kids have outgrown that activity, but I haven't.

Go ahead, be silly, go climb a tree.

Fairly recently, my 17 year old daughter was looking through some photos and she said, "Wow dad. We did some pretty cool trips when we were little. And I don't remember all of them."

I said, "Ya, we went everywhere. We canoed canyons, and we hiked small mountains, and we camped in some glorious forests. We rock-climbed Squamish and other great places and kayaked the Pacific Northwest with the seals. You guys were young and high maintenance out in the great outdoors, but it never seemed like effort. Well, ok, there were a few ski trips when you were little bitty that were a royal pain."

Trying to do a ski trip as the only adult with 2 little kids, skis, helmets, gloves, lift tickets – all of that. Ya, those trips were work. I knew then the kiddos wouldn't remember the details from those trips, but I also felt like: (a) the exposure to so many different adventures would make them comfortable with different situations, and (b) it gave me a chance to be in the great outdoors with the two folks I most love.

Now, we never did the Disney type stuff – that just wasn't my cup of tea with the crowds and the concrete and all. But getting away from the normal setting of the home seemed like a good idea then, and it still does. Even though I love to tease my kids about the fact I schlepped them all over God's creation, to some of the most beautiful natural sites on this continent, and they don't remember any of it. I tell them I could have just as well hung out at the house, and they wouldn't have known any better. I tease them for sure, but I don't really believe that.

What I'm talking about here is time with your kids. We did great adventures because I like great adventures. I like to create great adventures for myself. But when the kids are small, a great adventure can be a walk in the park. When the kids are small, that stick you step over is not a stick. It's a snake or it's a sword or it's a light saber. Adventures come in all sorts, large and small, with kids.

I remember just how high maintenance kids can be on adventure trips. We once took a canoe trip through Black Canyon, putting in at the base of Hoover Dam. On that trip, my 5 year old son had one of his heroic thoughts. His kindergarten class had this stuffed lion mascot, "Leopold the Lion". Each kid took Leopold home over the weekend and then returned on Monday to tell of what adventures Leopold had that weekend. Well, we were "fortunate" enough that Leopold's weekend with us happened to fall on spring break. I tried to convince my son we should leave Leo at home and not take him on that canoe trip, but my boy insisted the lion was to be with us the whole time. So, Leopold boarded a plane to Las Vegas. I thought it would be great if my son simply told the teacher we took the lion to Vegas, as a good luck charm for his dad. But then I thought, I don't know, perhaps not every teacher shared my sense of humor.

Leopold accompanied us to Hoover Dam and launched with us in that canoe, sitting at the aft as kind of masthead. The first day or two went seamlessly well, and on the 3rd day of camping we decided to hike to a hot spring I'd heard about. It fed a small steam bath. We began the hike, and all was going well. Under the top of the bluff, my son dropped the stuffed animal, and it had the temerity to let gravity take control. Ol' Leo tumbled down that bluff and off the edge of a 50' cliff into the river. Man, I can still see that damn lion tumbling in slow motion. We retraced our steps back toward the cliff, and we laid down to peer over the edge. And there sat Leopold. I guess he wasn't really sitting as much as he was swimming. Fortunately, he was caught in an eddy and was pushed up against the cliff by the current.

"I'll get him!" My boy informed, as he tore off down that steep canyon trail.

"Ah, it might be a better idea if we hike back to camp and see if we can use the fishing pole to catch him," I said.

That cliff was 40-50' high, and the water coming out of the base of Hoover Dam is about 40 degrees. Ten minutes or so in that water and hypothermia sets in. Sometimes, as a parent, you're caught between thinking your kids are the bravest people on the planet and total dumb asses.

So there we were, leaning over the cliff's edge, fishing for a lion. We hauled him up, and we went on to the hot spring. For a bit there, I thought we were going to have to launch the canoe and paddle downstream to retrieve that wayward animal.

My kids remember little of that trip, but they both remember me trying to get close enough to a rattlesnake to get a good photo. And they both remember the adventures of "Leo the swimming lion". I remember tons from that trip and every adventure we ever had. So go ahead. Take them everywhere. Create memories. Adventure feeds the soul.

Also, while you're on these trips, and even at the house, don't chastise for spilling their drinks or ice cream or whatever. Their hands are small, and they're getting the hang of this gravity thing. Let them try out every frickin' thing on the menu, even though you know it will taste like ass and they won't eat but one bite. How else will they ever find out if they like chitlins or escargot or neither? How else will they evolve an adventurous spirit?

Divorced Dads' Rule #27:
ALLOW YOUR KIDS TO WEAR NEW SHOES.

Remember when you were a teen and allow your kids to wear new shoes. Let me explain.

One summer day, while at my son's baseball game, I found myself involved in a conversation with my 15 year old daughter. "You know, I thought I would have noticed the eclipse."

"What eclipse, dad?"

"Well, the one that must have surely occurred when the planets stopped revolving around the Sun and started revolving around you," I calmly responded.

"You're ridiculous," she said.

"No. No actually, you are ridiculous. But I get it babe, and I've been waiting for this to happen for a long time. You see, you used to ask the most brilliant questions. Now, you have all the answers, and anybody who as much as disagrees with you is an idiot. You say they just don't get it."

She had no comment back. I put my arm around her and I said, "Look babe. I love you, and these new shoes are going to be interesting for the two of us. And I just hope we can do a better and more elegant job than most in adapting and dancing in these new shoes."

By the way, we did, and we didn't. And I put most of the blame when we didn't on me. But more on that later. Go back and read what Gibran says about raising children. That passage may better prepare you for the teen years.

I can remember when my younger sister was ready to go off to college. Now she was the youngest of eight kids, and my folks had been in the parenting business for over 30 years. It was time for her to fly the nest, and the whole deal was emotionally charged for my mom and for my baby sister. Now, there's been plenty written about the turmoil parents go through when faced with empty nest syndrome, not the least of which is reacquainting with the spouse. So the last kiddo, or maybe the only kiddo, leaves the nest, and the parents are faced with this "Holy crap – my identity has been wrapped up in being a parent all these years" crisis. And now, I don't even know who I am, and who the hell is this other person I've been married to all this time? Cause I've identified them as the other parent for so long, I've forgotten who they really are.

Some say all change is loss, but there is a richness to be had within you if you just look at the next chapter of your life as an adventure. Better yet, look at every chapter of your life as the next great adventure. You will no doubt be better served by not identifying yourself as a parent and projecting – what I'm talking about here is not living your life through your kids. Just accept that one role you play in this grand comedy called life is being a parent. There are plenty of other roles you can and should play in life. And in doing this, you might see the parenting role is actually a supporting actor role, not the lead role of your life.

Back to my sister flying the familial coop. She and mom had a devil of a time at the end. They started out bickering like teens and parents do. Then, it spiraled into a cold war of non-communication. It seemed they went through an extended time of simply not speaking to one another. I observed this dynamic for about a year. Most of my siblings and I tried to get my sister to re-engage with our mom. She was having none of it. And to be honest, she was only half the problem. Mom was contributing her fair share as well. Finally, after about a year of this, I had a chance to talk to my sister about this situation and a potential solution. I told her it was my observation that her schism with mom was necessary for the two of them. I went on to say I thought the two of them were so close and spent so much time together and had such a great influence on one another that there was no way my sister could come into her own womanhood without some cataclysmic split. It was necessary. The only way the two could let go was to actually go at one another and build a case against the other. This temporary vilification allowed the other, on an unconscious level at least, the ability to split. Hell, it may have even fed the need to split and be apart – sort of a reinforcement of the feeling of "hey, good riddance."

I encouraged my sister to look deep in her heart and to look back at her past with mom and see how close they really were – to recognize this was no aberration. Their co-created schism was necessary to allow her and mom to fit into their respective new shoes. But the split was ultimately not healthy for either of them, and it damn well made family get-togethers a bit of a drag. I went on to suggest that she would have to be the one to extend the olive branch, as mom probably didn't recognize what was going on. I also thought that neither my sister nor I could ever comprehend the incredible force of psychic energy of stepping out of parenting shoes after 34 years and how powerful the fear must be driving mom's action. I suggested to my baby sister that she only had 18 years of this mom-child dance, and since her invested time was only about half of mom's, she would have to be the one to eat the glass on behalf of a healthier relationship.

Years have gone by, and frankly I don't recall whether or not my sister took my advice. But she and mom are very close now. The healing of that relationship has benefited us all, and my sister's kiddos are all the better because their mom and their grandma have such a powerful bond.

Well, that story would be a good one to remember, and I wish I had recollected it when dealing with my own kiddo. When it was time for my first kid to put on her new shoes of independence, I believe I held on a little too long. My girl and I are good now. Hell, we're great now. It did take us about a year to sort through that evolutionary process. But I do believe, and she has confirmed this, we got through it relatively unscathed. Neither she nor I will need therapy for that period of her development. Not every kid gets through that stage of their lives without a tremendous amount of upheaval and damage. For this, my daughter and I are blessed.

It was easy raising kids in separate homes in different zip codes when they were little ones. But as they hit the teen years, specifically in our case around age 15, that lifestyle became more of a challenge. Their mom had primary custody, but we did about a 60/40 split, as I wanted be part, not of just weekends, of that every day school experience. You know, it seemed like all of a sudden, when my daughter turned 15, she disappeared from the face of my earth. I tried in vain to coerce her to spend time at my house. I even did the weekend beach house with friend invites to make sure I got some face time with her. But try as I might, there was always a reason for her to miss time with ol' dad. Now this period did offer an opportunity for me to get even closer with my son, and that was great. But I missed my girl, and I missed being a part of her world, and I missed her being a part of my world. I was also very concerned – hey I was downright fearful – that my positive influence on her might be dramatically diminished during these important teen years. After a year of this, I made a big decision. If Mohammed wasn't going to come to the mountain, I would move that damn mountain to Mohammed.

I got together with both my kiddos, and I made the announcement. "Guys, living in separate zip codes was easy when ya'll were little. I controlled the situation, and I got to call the shot when you came to the house. This last year has been a bit rough. You both seem to have developed this thing called a social life. I completely understand, and I accept. I actually want you to have that aspect of your life. You need that aspect of your life. But I am not good with the fact that it causes me to see you both so infrequently. So I'm going to make some changes. I'm going to rent out our home here, and I'm moving out near your mom."

In retrospect, this was a very good move, I believe. This was a great move. And for the first time in my life, parenting came at a cost. Before, all the sacrifices I had made as a parent seemed minimal. This one seemed a bit tough for me. I loved my old home in the Memorial Park area of Houston. And we fashioned a very nice home for ourselves in that old house. We'd lived there for over 12 years. Additionally, I was involved with a lady, and quite honestly was in love with her, and I was interested in making a lifelong journey with her. She lived and worked very close to our old home, and I knew moving out to the burbs was going to put our deal at risk. It did. Again, in retrospect, the move was a good idea, but it came at a cost. It came at a cost to me.

For the first six to eight months of living out in the burbs, my son was with me constantly. My evil scheme was working. My notion of the perfect rent house was based upon an observation I had made as a teenager. When I was in 9th grade, a girl in our high school, Janie, had the coolest house. Her parents were the coolest parents, and we all hung out at Janie's on weekends. I remember saying thanks to her dad for allowing us to hang out in their game room, doing nothing but playing ping pong and shooting pool. His response made an impression on me that exists to this day. "Pat," he said, "I actually want you guys hanging around here on the weekends. You see, every night you are here, I know where my daughter is, and I can observe her friends. While I'm not coming up to the game room very often, don't think I'm not watching what kind of kids are coming over to my house. The only rules we have around here, and you know them, are: (1) no booze or drugs, and (2) no sex. You guys respect that, and you keep each other in line, out of respect for me and my wife or because you don't want to lose the right to come over here. Believe me, this is a great situation for a parent. When ya'll are here, I know my daughter is not riding around boozing it up in a car or with someone who is. Even though at times I wish you all weren't as loud as you are, at least I know where my girl is, and I know who she is hanging out with." A wise man was Janie's dad. God rest his soul.

Well, in an effort to always learn from someone else's experience, I put together a list of criterion for our rent house.

- No more than 10 minutes from the high school.
- No more than 10 minutes from their mom's house.
- A pool.
- Enough space for the kids to hang out without feeling crowded.
- No more than 10 minutes from the nearest freeway back in to town.

Hey, I still need to get my fix of the inner loop lifestyle so that freeway proximity was for me. I've lived in the burbs before, and I knew it was no place for this single man. I found a crappy old house on 4 acres. It had a pool, and amazingly, it fit my parameters. Papers were signed. The deal was done. Moving was a bitch. I had some real emotional baggage to deal with around that, and I didn't even realize it at the time. In retrospect, I guess it was leaving a place I truly loved, coupled with the fear of not knowing if I was ever going back home. The fear of how all this might affect the relationship with my lady, and the fear that perhaps this experiment may not work at all. I could be left out in the burbs alone, with neither my kids nor my lady. But the die was cast and off I moved.

My son, as I said before, practically moved in right away. He was 14 and the notion of a safe place for him seemed to very much fit his needs. The house took on the look and feel of a college crash pad. Now, we had no less than three guitars and three amplifiers in the den, cables running everywhere, foot pedals all over the place, a swimming pool in the backyard, and ping pong table on the back porch. Four acres for them to roam around in and a fire pit out back for them to burn stuff. And Lord, do teenage boys love to burn stuff! I can still recall, just after we moved in, my son calling me to tell me he was pretty sure he could devise a fireproof float to allow that fire pit to be placed in the swimming pool and ignited. I told him I greatly appreciated his engineering genius, but that since we rented this place, burning it down the first month might show bad form. He argued back that it would look really cool at night to have that fire pit floating in the pool, and I argued back that he could do that in his own home when he was an adult. No doubt he will.

It was summer when we moved in, and it seemed like every morning I'd awake to make coffee and step over anywhere from three to five sleeping 15 year old boys. In the kitchen, I'd find the dog eating pizza, as she had pulled the box off the countertop. These mornings made me feel very comfortable in my decision to move. I had peace around it. I had created that safe space I had designed, and I believed my kids would be all the better for it.
My daughter took some time to come around, and it was only through more release by me that I believe she finally came home to us. It took faith and effort on my part and a continual reminder that she was exactly where she needed to be in her developmental process. And the most optimal move for me was to let her be, to let her dance in her shoes.

I can recall my frustration, which to me is an indication of my fears around loss of control. That is, after all, what all of this is about. I remember once saying to her, and believing in my heart then and now, that we would have handled this dynamic, this dance from dependence to independence to interdependence, differently than all others. I can vividly recall telling her, "You know, I knew this time would come – this point of separation in our daddy-daughter dance. But I thought we were close enough that we would handle it more elegantly." In that, I was wrong. We were indeed close enough, but that closeness caused the need for some break to be created – a break to allow her to dance off without me as her partner, at least not in the manner in which I was before.

As I said before, after about a year, she did come around. Maybe it would be better stated if I said "we" came around. As surely, it took growth and faith and patience on my part to let go enough for her to turn around to us. Her return to us was glorious, so much so that no sooner did she reappear on my radar screen she was asking me to meet her for lunch or dinner and even went so far as to ask if I was interested in taking ballroom dancing lessons with her. Me, ballroom dancing? Wow! I did it – ballroom dancing lessons, two nights a week. Talk about an opportunity to get face time with your kid. We would end up riding together and talking, and some evenings we'd even catch a meal before or after class. Obviously we had plenty of laughs while stepping on each other's feet. Those moments on that dance floor will be remembered and cherished by me forever. They ended too soon. She graduated from high school and worked two summer jobs getting ready for college. But those memories are etched in my soul. We will always have those memories of dancing and laughing together. I have those memories, those cherished memories of hanging out and laughing with my 17 year old college-bound daughter. Dancing offered an elegant manner for the two of us to reconnect. I also knew the time was short as she was soon to depart for college, which made me cherish those dance lessons all the more. The symbolism found in the fact that she wanted to renew our father-daughter dance with dance lessons was not lost in me. Ah, and the cosmos smiles, as all is as it should be, ever was, ever will be.

Once back together, it was as if we had never parted ways, save for the fact that when we reunited in our dance, we were both wearing different shoes. Gone were the daddy-little girl shoes, replaced with dad-young adult daughter shoes. It's a gas to have an adult conversation with your children – conversations filled with mutual respect even at points of dissention, conversations filled with honesty and openness, conversations filled with integrity for both partners. I no longer carry her. We carry ourselves, and we dance on. Dependence to independence to interdependence. And we dance on.

When the time comes for the kids to step into their own shoes and separate from the parents, my best advice is to let go as much as you possibly can. Remember what Karl Jung said, and again I paraphrase here, that the worst sin a parent can lay on a child is parental projection. Don't live your life through them. Realize you are only there to guide and nurture and set an example. By all means, listen to what Kahlil Gibran said and realize they are not yours. These kids, our kids are on loan from God, and our job as a parent is to work ourselves out of a job. If you don't believe this, then you'd better start saving two funds for your children – one a college fund and the other a therapy fund for all the damage you will do with your parental projection. Trying to live your unfulfilled life through your kid is singularly the most damaging thing you can do to another human being. The beauty is, and I believe this is true in all relationships, you just let go of that need to control the outcome. If you do so, you will free the other to live the life they want or need. Let go, and trust in the bond you established when they were little ones. Let go, and trust in the healing power of love. Perhaps, this is one of life's best opportunities to learn what the Buddhists talk about – "the sound of one hand clapping". For I believe that "the sound of one hand clapping", that non-opposition to force, the letting go of attachment to outcome – that's the message. Just letting go.

Speaking to that, I did execute with excellence in one point of this dance with my daughter. When she returned to us, I didn't say anything about her absence. We just picked up where we left off. It's been amazing, as it was before.

All this being said, there are parameters you believe in, and they should be reinforced with your children at all times. During those times when my daughter was absent from my world, I still let her and her mom know that unacceptable behavior was not going to occur without some comment from me. They knew when I encountered behavior which I found unacceptable, I at least communicated such. During that year away from us, while she was at her mom's house and not part of our world, I knew I had little influence on her actions and behaviors. This was a tough test for me, to be sure. I did, however, always let them know where I stood on the issues. Consistency and integrity are paramount to great parenting. You still must hold on to that line of integrity you have established. Consistency is the key, remember that. You may feel you are having little influence in the moment, and indeed this may be true. But at least you are reinforcing your commitment to parenting with integrity. Consistency at all times.

The bottom line is this. Let them try on their new shoes. Encourage them to try on their new shoes. They may stumble. They will stumble. But those are their lessons to learn. Just be there to catch them when they fall.

Divorced Dads' Rule #28:
TEACH THEM TO FOLLOW THEIR PASSION.

Every once in a while, I've remind my kiddos I didn't grow up as a little boy in southeast Houston dreaming of being a technology salesman. I had other dreams. I had dreams of being a national park ranger and spending my days and nights outside taking in some of nature's greatest displays. Hell, at one point I had dreams of being a professional football player. My path, since just after college, was to go the corporate route, and I'm okay with the "choices" I've made. I put the word "choice" in quotes because at the time, it wasn't such a conscious choice. Hey, I'm good at what I do, and it's afforded me a comfortable lifestyle. It's afforded me free time and countless trips aboard and trips to those national and state parks to enjoy nature's grandeur. It hasn't, however, been a career choice that has had me living my passion. I have over time moved more and more of my energy into my passions – the outdoors, photography, and perhaps even this little book. But on a day-in and day-out business, I've not been sitting in air-conditioned, Formica tabled, neon lit meeting rooms, and thought, "wow, this is it!".

I've told my children time and again that if ol' dad hasn't given up the dark socks and shined shoes by the time they all are done with college, then don't believe a word I've ever said to them. I've told them if I am not following my passion after I've satisfied my obligations to them, then I am indeed a fraud. Actually, this is my sneaky way of putting a gun to my own head and saying, "Nobody move or the sheriff gets it!" Forcing my hand so to speak.

Following their passion and staying true to themselves are great directions to offer your offspring. That's a gift you can give your kids, and that's a gift you can give the planet. One night at the dinner table, my daughter spoke out in frustration. She was in the gifted and talented program at school and frustrated over trying to keep up with the brainiacs. Never mind that gifted and talented tag drove me crazy, I mean, what the hell, which child, which human is not gifted and talented in some way? But tags are tags, aren't they?

She said, "Daddy, I'm tired of the smarties in my class making fun of my questions. I mean I can change who I am so they think I'm smarter or I can be more popular and all, but I hate it when they make fun of me for not being as smart as they are."

"Don't ever change who you are for someone else." Knowing, at this moment, we had a great parenting opportunity. "Every time you change who you really are for someone else, you are letting go of a piece of you. And that you, that whole you, is the greatest gift you can give the world. Don't ever put yourself in a place where you are giving less than your entire self to this world. Guys, that's a gift *you* give in return for the great gifts life has given you."

Going on even further, "Giving up you, even a little bit, puts you on a path to give up a bit more the next time. We call that compromise. And while compromise in some cases is okay, it's never okay when you're compromising on that which is most important to you. You see baby, that changing who you really are for others deal, it's kind of like putting on a mask and wearing that mask for other people. The problem is that while you're wearing that mask, you're not wearing your true shoes. You're not being your true self. And I can tell you that this world is full of people who are walking around in shoes other than the ones that are truly theirs. They are wearing somebody else's shoes. They are wearing shoes somebody else has put on them. They are not living a life of integrity. It's as if they have allowed other people to put different shoes on them – their parents, their teachers, their grandparents, their friends, the braniacs at school, or other people. The biggest problem with this is that eventually you realize you are walking around, or maybe even stumbling around, in somebody else's shoes. You realize you're not happy in these shoes because they don't really fit you. Then you realize that for you to be really happy in life, you have to change shoes now and put on your true shoes. The real problem here is that you've been walking around in those shoes for so long you've forgotten what your true shoes feel like. It will take a long time because of your fear, and because everyone else wants you to stay in the shoes they've put on you. But you know you will not be really happy until you start walking or dancing in your true shoes. This is a huge problem for many adults."

How else do you describe a midlife crisis to kids?

I went on to talk to them both at the dinner table about midlife crises, and how to change that from a crisis to a passage and, hopefully, to move that up in the batting order of life so you don't have to wait to midlife to wear the right shoes. I told them the most optimal manner of living life is to always stay in your true shoes and to live your life for yourself – to recognize and chase your own passion, not one that someone else has pushed on you. I went on to explain that my life choices were okay for me, but that I had found myself immersed in obligations: house, cars, kids, wife etc. I couldn't find a way out of that corporate life without walking away from those obligations. I went on that a more optimal choice might be to follow your passion before you encumber yourself with financial and other obligations. I explained it may be far easier to move to the corporate world later in life, if that was a choice, than to walk away once you're obligated.

So far, so good. Neither of my kiddos have designs on being in the corporate world. Very possibly, very probably, they may struggle financially at the onset of their adult life as they chase their respective passions. What the hell? Most of us struggle financially at the beginning anyway – sometimes at the middle and the end. I hope they continue to pursue their passions – dramatic arts for my daughter and music for my son. But I can also let go of their choices. If they do choose the dark socks and dry cleaned clothes route, then that's their challenge with which to deal. Responsibility for their actions is part of their wearing authentic, true shoes.

I can recall an early morning phone call from my ex-wife. "Your son says he's too sick to go to school. Can you talk to him?" she asked.

"Does he have a fever? Is he throwing up?"

"No, will you please talk to him?" she said.

I told my son that if he didn't have a fever, but couldn't go to school, then he could just get dressed up and spend the day with me. He was 15 at the time, and frankly I thought that just getting dressed up to go to my office would be painful enough to get his butt to school. He agreed to go with me to the office. He must have had a test that day. It had to be one of the most boring days of his life. It was January, and I was going over the new year's goals and plans with my employees. He sat in my office for 8 hours while one after another after another of my employees came in and sat down and went over their objectives and plans for the year.

On the way home I mentioned that I hoped my devious plan had worked. And that he had seen enough of the corporate world to know that he wanted another path for himself. As he got into the car, he said, "You know, you didn't have to do this to keep me from going into the corporate world. I already know that I don't want to do that." That night at dinner he said without looking up from his plate, "You know, you don't work very hard."

"What's your point?" I asked without looking up from my steak-filled plate.

"I mean, all you did was drink coffee all day and talk to people."

"Well, that's what I do. And once you get your college degree, you can have that glorious life if you want it."

"Hey, no thanks. There's no way I want to sit around and talk to my friends all day, much less people I don't even hang out with," he said.

Perhaps my evil scheme had worked after all.

Divorced Dads' Rule #29:
MAKE THE HOME A SAFE PLACE.

I'm not talking about child locks on doors and cabinets and putting away all the toxic cleaning products. If you can't figure that out on your own, then your kids are doomed anyway. I'm talking about a safe place emotionally.

My kids couldn't be any different in personality types. My daughter is just like me. She is an extreme Type "A" personality and is forever goal-setting and goal-attaining to the point where she will wear herself out. Acceptance from others rates high on her needs list, and she' a bit of an enabler. Again, she's got a lot of her daddy in her. This is not all good and, obviously, not all bad. It just is. She's a high-achiever. She's performed on cruise ships as a young dancer. She won city and state writing awards. She's medaled in national dance competitions. She graduated #11 in her high school class in just 3 years of high school. She's received multiple college scholarships. All of this is due to that internal Type "A" drive.

Believe me – her mom and I spent many years trying to get her to take a breather from one activity or another. That is, until we finally realized she is just a force to be reckoned with. This is a kid who at 17 years old was diagnosed on a Friday afternoon with mono and worked a 10 hour shift the next day. "Hey, mind over matter" is what she always says. Too much, perhaps, of what drives her is about other people's perception of her. That and that damned enabler load she carries are going to be a real challenge for her. Now I know this from my own personal life, and I can see it in her life. Watching her live her life, at times, it's like looking in a long-haired mirror.

I've already witnessed her enabling ways with a boyfriend and other friends who were making poor choices in their lives. But again, she comes by that quite naturally. I just try to make sure she's aware of those causative agents and aware on a conscious level of her actions. I tell her time and again that I hope she gets over some of her challenges, specifically that co-dependence, that enabling aspect, in far fewer years than it's taken her dear old dad. Actually, I tell her I hope she gets through those challenges rather than gets over them – learning to live consciously around those deep seeded needs.

I recently told her I was 47 years old, and in my last relationship, I was caught up again in my lady's life struggles. And I took them on as my own, all to the detriment of that relationship. You can't take on somebody else's stuff and maintain the energy to live your life in the manner in which you should. Assisting a loved one is one thing, but taking on their stuff is no way to be a partner in a relationship. That is not assisting or supporting, but rather enabling. "I was 47", I told her, "and I am still doing it."

I hope she can recognize these patterns in her life because they surely exist. And I hope she can get through it long before she turns 47. We'll see. That's her cross to bear. And all I can do is hold up a mirror for her and remind her that living an integrity-filled life is living a conscious driven life.

My son is pretty much the polar opposite of his sister and me. He is the archetypal maven and has all the characteristics of such. He doesn't care too much if you like him – he actually doesn't care at all if you like him. He's a jokester, but the jokes are for his amusement only. Life is for his amusement. He's damn near great at everything he puts his mind and hands to and that is a double-edged sword. His sister and I have to work hard at whatever endeavors in which we engage. He, on the other hand, seems to be great at whatever he tries. His life challenge, I believe, will be to develop the discipline and rigor to stick with something once he surpasses his natural gifts. And his challenge is to become the true master. Or not! As it is his life to live.

The difference in personality between my son and me has been one of my most enjoyable challenges as a parent. If I hadn't spent a career in technology, working around programmers and geophysicists, I might not have been prepared for that challenge. You see, with my daughter, it was always easy to understand the drivers of her actions. Almost surely, those same drivers had affected my life at one time or another. With my boy, there was always a need to get into his head, for me to put on my empathy shoes or for me to swap shoes, and to walk around in his shoes so I could better understand where he was coming from or why he was doing what he was doing.

I can recall meeting with a math teacher back in his 2nd grade year. She was all concerned about my son's work. We sat down at a table, and she pulled out three different students' work. The first was a beautiful art exhibit. Remember, this was math class. It was a winter wonderland all done in shaded colored pencil. It showcased a decorated Christmas tree or two, snow bunnies, a smattering of snowmen, etc. Strewn across that scene was a sidewalk with math facts inserted into the squares of the walkway. "This is not an example of your son's work," she said.

"No, I didn't think it was," I replied smiling.

The next example was the same math facts, but instead of a sidewalk, they were the body of a snake with this menacingly fanged head complete with exposed forked tongue and all. The tail even had a rattle. "This is another boy's work," she said.

The next example was the same math facts, but in between each math fact was a red squiggly line. Imagine, if you will, taking a red Sharpie pen and haphazardly striking a line between each math fact. "This is your son's work," she informed.

"Oh," I replied.

Long uncomfortable pause…………..

"It's a candy cane," she finally confirmed.

"Oh! Okay," I replied.

"Okay? Okay? Do you think this work is okay, Mr. Talley?" she asked.

"No, no, no! I was just saying okay because I didn't know what the heck it was! And now I know at least it's a candy cane!" I said.

"So what do you think of this work, Mr. Talley?" she asked.

"Ma'am," I began, "is his math correct?" I asked.

"Yes, he never misses any problems, but his work is rushed and haphazard at best," she explained.

"Well, now I think I can see the problem." She gave me a look of pleasure. She'd finally gotten to me. She'd finally gotten me to a point of understanding that we indeed had a problem.

I began, "Well, I can tell you that the first picture, that winter wonderland picture, was done by a girl. And it looks like the work that my daughter would have done. She is very interested in pleasing teachers. But my son, all due respect ma'am, he could care less if you like him. As a matter of fact, he could care less what you think of him at all. Getting the math problems or challenges correct, that's something he does care about. But it's pure intrinsic motivation for him. He will never, ever do work to please you or me. But he will do more work and harder work if you give it to him, as he accepts that intellectual challenge. He may do interesting art work in art class, but probably cannot even comprehend the need to do interesting art in math class. Besides, if you or I or any of his other teachers put emotions into him doing things for us, then I think we're going to all be let down. My suggestion is that you give him hard math challenges, and simply realize he will respond to that and not much more."

She didn't seem to like my reaction, so I tried to be a bit more gentle with her. "Ma'am, it's taken me some time to understand that this kid is not like me. I would have been the kid who tried to please you with the pretty picture in math class. I'm a lot like my daughter. This guy is simply not wired that way. And if we try to project our personality type and that production onto him, it will only end in frustration for us, because I know for a fact he's not going to change his stripes. Nor should he, I believe," I said closing that conversation. He makes very good grades. He puts in almost zero effort at it. He's bored with the speed of the classroom. He's aced every state standardized test for the past 7 years or so. But he does not put in any extra effort to have the teachers like him any more than the other students.

I've had talks with him to make certain he recognizes this aspect of his personality. Now, I've tried to explain to him that society has a given set of unwritten and unspoken rules, and most people abide by these rules, and most people expect you to abide by these rules. More importantly, they expect all others to abide by these rules. They may judge you harshly if you don't play by those rules. I've told him that his "in-your-face" honesty doesn't play well with most people; and that as much as he detests the charade of looking a stranger in the eye and firmly shaking their hand, some folks will judge him unfavorably because he acts with disinterest in those situations. I tell him he can play things his way, or he can play things by others' rules, and it's his choice. But he must certainly recognize that by not playing the game, he will encounter obstacles that he could avoid if he would just play the game.

Regardless of the choices he makes, I tell him the number one rule, for him, is to recognize and not complain about society's prejudice against his personality type. Again, I'm not trying to change his nature at all. He can live his life as he sees fit. I just want the guy to understand he can grease the skids if he plays the game. Or not. But, accepting the outcome of not playing is a move of true integrity – walking in his true shoes with style.

I've experienced his style for many years, and I have a few examples of just how frank a guy he can be. His honesty can be disarming at times. One time at the dinner table, he was about 10 or so, he looked up and he said, "Dad, this chicken is good and everything, but no offense, but the white sauce on these peas tastes like ass."

"Okay, okay, don't eat it, and I'm glad you like the chicken," I said thinking, you little shit, it took me 30 minutes to get that sauce right.

But that is my boy. To him, that is just being totally honest. He's not telling me he doesn't like me or he doesn't love me. He's not telling me he doesn't appreciate me making a family meal. He's just saying he doesn't like my white sauce.

More recently, we spent two days in Austin while visiting the campus where my daughter was about to launch her collegiate career. We went everywhere, and we saw everything that weekend. I took her all over the campus, all over the city. We looked around her dorm, we walked around the lake, and we got wet at Barton Springs. I even took her to a couple of Austin's more famous college crowd eateries.

My son, 15 at the time, accompanied us with designs on hooking up with one of his buddies who happens to live in Austin and who is also into playing guitars. They intended to play all weekend long. Now, that kid called us on the drive up and he bailed out as he had a fever. My boy ended up hanging out with us the entire weekend. He toured the campus, and he toured Austin.

As I was dropping them off at the end of the weekend, my daughter went into one of her gracious thank you spiels. "Thanks sooo much daddy, thank you, it was an awesome weekend. I really appreciated you showing me how to get to the lake and Barton Springs," she gushed.

Out of the back of the SUV came the following, "I don't want to be an ass or anything, but I feel like I just wasted two days of my life," my darling boy said.

"Well, it's a good thing you don't want to be an ass about it," my daughter shot back.

"Hey, girl," I said as I laid my hand on her leg to calm her down a bit. "That's just him being honest, he doesn't mean to offend, he's just telling me what he feels, and he knows it doesn't have anything to do with how much he cares for me or any of that stuff. He's just saying he didn't get what he wanted out the weekend. We're all going to have to learn he doesn't mean anything other than exactly what he is saying when he says things like that. He, on the other hand, may someday learn that keeping that stuff to himself may take him farther than not. But that's his deal, not ours. Let's hope someday he finds a nice lady or man, hey, whatever, who accepts his kind of declarations for what they are and not as an offense to them."

"Well, I can just see it now," my daughter began. "His wife is going to ask, 'honey, do these pants make my butt look fat?' To which he'll reply… 'nope, it ain't the pants, it's your fat butt.'"

I laughed and I laughed at that one, and I said, "Yep, you're probably right, babe. And bud, I'm glad you came with us. Now ya'll go spend some time with your mom. She probably missed ya'll."

I do feel the need to defend this guy for a minute. He's a heck of a young man. I've seen him being extremely gentle and extremely patient with little kids and with animals. And he always seems to have a soft touch for his grandparents and old folks in general. I recall one Halloween, when he was about nine years old, he was running the streets with his costumed buddies, and Jake, one of his friends' little brother, was trying to keep up. As they ran from one house to the next, Jake took a tumble. As he hit the ground, all of his Halloween candy went flying in the air. Seven of the older boys raced past, glancing over, but not slowing down to help. None of them stopped to help. Not even his brother. Raiding the next house of candy was a higher calling. My boy stopped, and very hurriedly started scooping up all of Jake's spilled candy and stuffing it back into the little guy's plastic jack-o-lantern. He then handed the candy-filled container back to Jake, and he took off like a shot to join his buddies. Not a word was said. No "thank you" was expected. That is simply my son's style.

Divorced Dads' Rule #30:
IT TAKES TIME TO BREAK IN NEW SHOES.

Realize that divorce delivers a new pair of shoes for your kids to put on. Pay attention and realize every move you make will have some impact. Do what you can to ensure the impact be a positive one.

Transition can be tough for some kids. Hell! Transition can be tough for all of us. My son is the kind of kid, who could be playing with a piece of string on the floor, and you walk in with an invitation to take him to Disneyworld, and he would just look up and say, "Nah, not right now." Whatever he was doing was far better than anything he could be doing next. He's pretty much still that way. He may fall into the category of someone who sees all change as loss.

My ex-wife and I really struggled with transitioning him from one house to the other. It was murder to get him into my SUV to go to my home for our time together. He would say no, then he would cry, then he would get argumentative. Hell! Sometimes he even got physically combative. Forget about how it felt to go through breaking up my family, now I was torturing my kid by making him go with me. Seeing that my own boy didn't want to be with me, I got all caught up in those histrionics. This was not the case at all, but it is how I felt. This was simply a matter of transitioning.

Now this was only a matter of changing shoes, and we needed a plan. The solution presented itself one day, and like most solutions, it came in a moment of calm. It was wholly unexpected, and it proved to be a rather elegant solution. We, for some logistical reasons, needed to meet at a grocery store rather than my ex-wife's house. Meeting at that neutral spot proved for a very easy transition for my boy. He had no problem hopping out of mom's SUV and into mine, where before he had a problem going from the home to the SUV. Once we realized this, we no longer yanked him from home to home, but instead, we transitioned at neutral spots like gas stations, grocery stores, or convenience stores. Perhaps, it was even more enticing a bit because they had snacks or drinks at those stores. Go ahead, think of this as conniving or bribery – I don't care. If it keeps tears out of your little guy's eyes, you'll do it too.

Also, it may be good for your kids to be around other divorced kids. This came to me again as a very unintentional coincidence. A friend invited me to go to the park with my kids and a few other families. When we arrived, I found that the other families were divorced moms and their children. It was a great picnic with lots of good food and lots of time with all these kids playing around. On the way back to our car, my daughter, who was all of five years old, said, "Daddy, I didn't know you knew so many divorced people."

The message was clear, and for once, I refrained from trying to make a lesson out of every conversation. She understood in that moment she wasn't alone. Other children had divorced parents, and they seemed to be happy kids, and they all played in the water just like normal kids.

I've proudly witnessed this as my son, as a teenager, would counsel his buddies who were distraught over their parents' pending divorces. Kids need to know everything is going to be all okay, and they are loved.

A long time ago, I heard discomfort in my daughter's voice as she told of a story, and I made a promise to myself and to both of my children then and there. In that moment, a vow was made. The vow gave them a safe haven. It was a promise that seemed to me to be very easy to make. At the time, I had no idea of the significance it would have on their comfort level.

My kids and I were playing on the rocks along a riverbed, and one of them mentioned that mom had a new boyfriend. I asked if they liked the guy. They said yes, and my son added, "I like him a lot because he buys me lots of stuff."

"Well, I'm glad you like the guy," I said.

Then my son added, "Well, I don't know if I really like him, but I like that he buys me stuff."

Out of the mouths of babes.

Then my kids went on to tell me this guy had a son in New Mexico and a daughter somewhere in Tennessee. I stopped cold in my tracks. They were trying to tell me something.

"Hey, let's sit down," I said. "I want you guys to understand something. Please, put on your listening ears. I'm your dad, I'm not going away. Your mom and I, we're divorced now, but I'm not going away – ever! I will always, always live in the same city as you. If your mom were to move to another city, I would be there in two days. If she moved to another city after that, I would follow forever. You guys don't have to worry about me not ever living in the same city as you. Do you get that?" I was firm in this delivery and looked them both in the eyes. They got it.

This was one of those few moments of parenting where I knew we were in the moment, and the dynamic had impact. The statement about the other guy and his kids in far-flung states was mentioned with tension in my daughter's voice. That resolute answer I gave put us all back on track, and we happily hopped along those river rocks.

Since these are new shoes for your kids, you can bet they will test the waters to find out what it's all about. Rest assured. Every angle will be tested, unconsciously or otherwise. Be prepared, and be in the moment. Be in the moment to realize they are asking questions because they are trying to figure it all out. No question should be treated as idle or of little consequence in these moments of new shoes. And yes, they will test you to see if you are okay with mom moving on with her life. Your reaction may influence their reaction so be aware.

One time my kids and I were on a canoe camping trip. My daughter and I started dancing under the stars. She then said, quite out of the blue, "Mom goes dancing with Mr. Ron all the time."

"Hmm, I wonder why she'd never go dancing with me," I mused.

"Maybe she likes him more," she said.

"Maybe she does."

Long pregnant pause ensued. Then we both busted a gut laughing. Those canyon walls echoed with our laughter. Tension was released and my daughter understood without going into direct conversation on the topic that it was okay for her mom to spend time with someone else. It was okay, as far as I was concerned, and this released my daughter from worrying about how dad was going to react. She also, in that moment, understood that it was okay for her to like the new guy and that she was not betraying her dad by doing so. This, perhaps, somehow told her it was okay for her to be okay with Mr. Ron being around. Kids need reassurance to let them know it is okay to feel how they feel.

I believe in retrospect this situation was a clear case of my daughter testing those waters, to see how things work post-divorce. I wasn't really aware or conscious of the fact at the time. And looking back, that was clearly the case. The sense of tension that existed in her, as well as my release of that tension to laughter, indicated such to be the case. These shoes were becoming more comfortable for her and perhaps for me as well.

Divorced Dads' Rule #31:
SHOCK AND AWE CAN WORK FOR PARENTING, TOO.

Once, while taking a road trip to the Texas Hill country, my 11 year old son was sitting up front in the SUV and listening to his Sony Discman. My daughter and I were enjoying Dr. John on my CD player, and he was enjoying whatever it was he wanted. After an hour or so, I said to him, "Hey bud. Give me that CD, and we'll all enjoy it."

"Ah, that's okay, dad. I don't think you guys would like this stuff too much," was his reply.

"Naw, come on, give it up. I want to hear what you're listening to," was my still-innocent request.

"Naw, you won't like it," he urged with some amount of fear now in his voice.

"Okay, that nails it, give me the damn CD." The innocence was gone. He handed it over, and he squirmed a bit in his seat. I still didn't fully understand why. I popped the CD in after looking at the name on it. And I recollected that I knew Eminem but wasn't extremely familiar with his music.

Well, the first song was okay – it had okay lyrics and a good beat. The next song started off by dropping an "F bomb", which was followed by "motherfucker". My 11 year old son was squirming big time now. In my rearview I could see his sister delighted at the pending fireworks display. He squirmed on.

"Dad, we can just turn this off," he cried out.

"Nope, I want to hear what it is you like, pal," I calmly replied.

We listened to a few more songs as we rolled along Hwy 290, and then I said, "Man, I'm getting pretty hungry. Let's pull off and get some grub."

I didn't mention anything about that CD while we ate, and for the first time ever his appetite seemed to be closer to a normal human than a wolverine. As I recall it was a pretty quiet lunch. We got back in the SUV, and I popped the CD out and put in some John

Prine. We rolled for about 10 minutes, and then I shut off the CD player, and I said, "Bud, what's the word mom mean to you?"

He had no idea where I was going with this, but I did. He went on to explain that this is the woman who gives you birth and takes care of you and raises you, etc. Then I asked, "And what does the word mother mean to you?"

He was still clueless to our direction and gave basically the same answer. I continued, "So I'm sitting here trying to figure out how or why you would want to attach the word 'fucker' to your mother."

"Dad!" He almost jumped out of his seat.

"I mean, I'm trying to figure out why you would want that word attached to my mother, who is your grandmother."

"Dad, stop it! I wasn't thinking of anything like that!" He cried out. My rearview was showing that his sister was indeed enjoying this show – a perfect example of sheudenfreud if there ever was one.

"Look, here's the idea, bud. Words matter. I know you didn't write those lyrics, but you bought that CD, and you're the one listening to it. That means that somehow, someway, you're supporting someone who talks or sings like that."

Man, I was just getting ramped up.

I went on to explain what the word misogyny meant, and that those lyrics were misogynistic in nature, and that in some way he was supporting that whole female-hating mindset. At the very least, he was unconsciously going along with the deal. He assured me he was not, and I reminded him that words do indeed matter. I went on for a while, and he had finally had enough.

"Dad, we can just throw that CD in the trash. I will never listen to it again."

Now, as far as I know, this was the last time my son enjoyed Slim Shady. Pretty quickly he was over his rap fixation and into classic rock. Regardless of if this was a perfect parenting moment – it's not often I would suggest you drop "F bombs" in front of your preteens. But he'd opened that door, and I simply walked through it. And honestly, if it got him off rap and into classic and blues infused rock, then as far as I'm concerned, all the better.

Divorced Dads' Rule #32:
BE BOTH SUPERMAN AND CLARK KENT.

This is more a story of observation from another buddy's family. Ed is an old friend of mine. Ed is a strong man, both physically and in regard to integrity. He does the right things. Ed is an extreme self-starter. He's a hard worker and a very successful businessman. His teen son seemed to be stuck with the "what the hell do I do with my life" question. It appeared the boy was stagnant. It appeared to me he was stagnant due to fear. It also seemed to me that a big part of this boy's fears revolved around that fear of never being successful enough to measure up.

I thought about this situation, and I came to a few conclusions. Ed is a strong man. Ed is a strong man in a physical sense, as he is a former competitive powerlifter, a national champion as a matter of fact. He's still very large physically and very formidable. As I said before, he's also an extremely successful businessman. He's an expert hunter, and he's bagged big game all over this continent. I realized, thinking in "oedipal" terms, this is a real conundrum. Here's a kid who feels he will never be able to kill the father figure. There is a need to break free, and somehow, in someway surpass the father archetype. However, in a man of Ed's stature and strength, this seemed a near impossible task. So the kid just simply locked up.

Ed and I, after several conversations about this, came to the conclusion that while he had been doing his job playing the role of father, he had never let his kid see him sweat. This left his son with the false impression that his father was Superman, a superhuman, and with feelings that no matter how great his own successes could be, they would never surpass the father. So why even try?

Ed and I came upon a plan where he would find some alone time with his son, working around the house or the yard or whatever. And in that time, Ed would make certain that his son knew that as strong a man, as successful a man as he was, Ed still had fears – fears that all dads have, fears that all men have, fears that all humans have, fears about not being able to guarantee his family's health, fear that his next big business venture would crater and stagger his commercial progress, fears that he could get sick and die. It seemed to Ed and to me that his son most probably assumed that dad was this superhero who never questioned himself and who never feared failure. Obviously, Ed's life was like all successful men. It was fraught with fear, but he lived it by embracing and taking on those fears. His son had never smelled a whiff of fear on his dad, and therefore, his own fears seemed to be daunting, stifling even. After all, if his role model of a man had never shown fear, then how strong could the son possibly perceive himself to be if every day he felt the fear of failure in his life?

I'm not sure if this conversation relieved any of psychic shackles that held this kid back. But after that conversation, the kid seemed to get on track. He got a job in another city. He moved, got his own apartment. He seems to be doing a good job of stepping into his own shoes – his shoes of manhood.

This dynamic taught me to make sure my kids did not see their dad as a fearless world-beater, but rather as a man who strides on, not in spite of his fears, but to some degree, due to his fear recognition, and a man who embraces those fears. I've dialogued with my kids about this. They know fear can stall you out. They know fear exists. They know the way of the warrior, the way of the hero. The hero's path is to smell that fear, to recognize that fear, to turn and embrace that fear, and dance with that fear. It is all about choice and actions.

I think some folks get caught up in negatively judging a man when he expresses his fears. I've seen ladies do this in the past. They, at times, have some romantic notion of me as hero. Me as their hero is an unrealistic notion to be certain. Then, when I express fear, they see it as a sign of weakness, and that hero tumbles from the "projected" pillar. I can tell you I measure a man in a different manner. To me a brave man has nothing to do with quaking at the entrance to the dragon's lair. No, to me, the measure of a real man is that when he encounters that cave entrance, he may even be so scared that he pees on himself, but in spite of that fear, he draws his "vorpal" sword, and he enters that cave and goes after that damn dragon. Now that is a man! I want my children to know that dad has fears. He has fears every day, but he recognizes and he even embraces them. And he presses on in spite, or perhaps to spite, his fears.

Divorced Dads' Rule #33:
**THE ROAD TO HELL IS PAVED WITH GOOD
INTENTIONS.**

Mom was and is a tough old bird. She raised eight kids, five sons and three daughters and buried one son. She is a former ER nurse and shows her best side when the chips are down and the shit is hitting the fan. She is as cool as the other side of the pillow, as they say.

She always hammered into us "the road to hell is paved with good intentions". This is a damn harsh lesson to learn as a kid but a true gift to realize as an adult. There is no room in my mom's world for "I was gonna do this" or "I wanted or intended to do that". For mom, it is and always has been all about actions. Your intentions are not what you should be measured upon but rather your actions. This, I believe is an elegant way to teach integrity.

Thanks mom!

Divorced Dads' Rule #34:
PRINT A COPY OF KAHLIL GIBRAN'S "ON THE
CHILDREN" TAKEN FROM HIS BOOK THE
PROPHET.

TEAR OUT THE FOLLOWING PAGE.
TAPE IT TO YOUR BATHROOM MIRROR.

"ON THE CHILDREN"
Taken from <u>The Prophet</u> by Kahlil Gibran

You may give them your love but not your thoughts,
For they have their own thoughts.
You may house their bodies but not their souls,
For their souls dwell in the house of tomorrow,
which you cannot visit, not even in your dreams.
You may strive to be like them, but seek not to make
them like you.
For Life goes not backward nor tarries with yesterday.
You are the bows from which your children as living
arrows are sent forth.
The archer sees the mark upon the path of the infinite,
and He bends you with His might that His arrow may
go swift and far.
Let your bending in the archer's hand be for gladness;
For even as He loves the arrow that flies,
so He loves also the bow that is stable.

Divorced Dads' Rule #35:
GO BACK AND READ DIVORCED DADS' RULE #1.

TEAR OUT THE FOLLOWING PAGE.
USE AS A REFERENCE IF YOU SO CHOOSE.

Divorced Dads' Rules

Divorced Dads' Rule #2:

GET DIVORCED AS FAST AS YOU CAN.

Divorced Dads' Rule #3:

CAVE IN ON EVERYTHING THAT IS NOT LIFE CHANGING.

Divorced Dads' Rule #4:

TELLING THE KIDS IS FAR MORE EMOTIONAL ON YOU THAN IT
IS ON THEM.

Divorced Dads' Rule #5:

THAT WHICH MOST DRIVES YOU CRAZY ABOUT YOUR WIFE
WILL CONTINUE TO DRIVE YOU CRAZY AS YOU RAISE
CHILDREN.

Divorced Dads' Rule #6:

GO GET LAID!

Divorced Dads' Rule #1:

NEVER UTTER A DISCOURAGING WORD ABOUT YOUR KIDS'
MOM.

Divorced Dads' Rule #7:

YOUR EX-WIFE'S FRIENDS AND FAMILY WON'T BE YOUR
FRIENDS AND FAMILY.

Divorced Dads' Rule #8:

DON'T HIT YOUR KIDS.

Divorced Dads' Rule #9:

GO FIND A CHILD REARING MENTOR.

Divorced Dads' Rule #10:

GIVE THE GIFTS TO THE KIDS.

Divorced Dads' Rule #11:

EAT LOTS OF GLASS FOR YOUR KIDS.

Divorced Dads' Rule #12:

QUALITY OVER QUANTITY IS BULLSHIT!

Divorced Dads' Rule #13:

DON'T MISS THE CHILD SUPPORT CHECKS – EVER!

Divorced Dads' Rule #14:

BE THE PARENT IN YOUR HOME, AND ENCOURAGE YOUR KIDS'
MOM TO BE THE PARENT IN HER HOME.

Divorced Dads' Rule #15:

GIVE THEM THE BIG HEAD.

Divorced Dads' Rule #16:

DON'T SAY "NO" WHEN YOU CAN SAY "YES".

Divorced Dads' Rule #17:

INCORPORATE THE "RULE OF 3'S" INTO YOUR LIFE.
Divorced Dads' Rule #18:
GO BUY A FLOWERED APRON.
Divorced Dads' Rule #19:
BE A HOMEROOM DAD.
Divorced Dads' Rule #20:
BE THE COACH.
Divorced Dads' Rule #21:
ACCEPT THAT YOU AND YOUR EX- WILL PARENT DIFFERENTLY.
Divorced Dads' Rule #22:
WHEN WITH YOUR CHILDREN, SAVE ENOUGH ENERGY TO BE IN THE MOMENT.
Divorced Dads' Rule #23:
READ SOMETHING, ANYTHING, ON A FREQUENT BASIS.
Divorced Dads' Rule #24:
SHUT DOWN THOSE PROJECTORS.
Divorced Dads' Rule #25:
TEACH YOUR CHILDREN ACCEPTANCE AND DIVERSITY.
Divorced Dads' Rule #26:
MAKE LASTING MEMORIES.
Divorced Dads' Rule #27:
ALLOW YOUR KIDS TO WEAR NEW SHOES.
Divorced Dads' Rule #28:
TEACH THEM TO FOLLOW THEIR PASSION.
Divorced Dads' Rule #29:
MAKE THE HOME A SAFE PLACE.
Divorced Dads' Rule #30:
IT TAKES TIME TO BREAK IN NEW SHOES.
Divorced Dads' Rule #31:
SHOCK AND AWE CAN WORK FOR PARENTING, TOO.
Divorced Dads' Rule #32:
BE BOTH SUPERMAN AND CLARK KENT.
Divorced Dads' Rule #33:
THE ROAD TO HELL IS PAVED WITH GOOD INTENTIONS.
Divorced Dads' Rule #34:
PRINT A COPY OF KAHLIL GILBRAN'S "ON THE CHILDREN" TAKEN FROM HIS BOOK THE PROPHET.
Divorced Dads' Rule #35:
GO BACK AND READ DIVORCED DADS' RULE #1.

Book Review

"Reading this book was a great experience. This guy writes with wonderful humor and keen insight into how we all process through life. His stories are insightful, compelling and darn funny. He cuts through the B.S. that other people seem to get engulfed in. Above and beyond everything else there is a huge degree of integrity in this writing. (Ben S. from New York City)

"Simply THE BEST parenting book that I have ever read! Divorced or not this book will help you handle your parenting challenges as the writer says "dancing elegantly in your shoes." Learn from his honest remembrances of times he did well and times that he claims to have "stumbled in HIS parenting shoes." (Adriana B. from Peru, S.A.)

"Every time I talked with Patrick, the subject of how to be an amazing Dad to our kids came up - it was just a natural part of our conversations. We'd share stories and the wisdom Patrick shared as he related his own conversations with his kids gave me insights into how I could have a deeper and more meaningful relationship with my own kids. I wouldn't trade those conversations for anything. This book will make a difference!" (J. Hotz from Bastop Texas)

"This book is for anyone that has ever had the guts to take a hard look in the mirror and re-evaluate his / her life. Patrick delineates an unshakable path to growth based on values, grace and truth. The stories unfold in effortless fashion while the learning opportunities magnify. Patrick's insights will empower you!" (M.G. from Louisiana)

"This book is so refreshing and thought-provoking. It is unique in that it does not set out the opinions and advice of a professional but rather those of an everyday dad (although in no way an average dad). It is a fresh, direct perspective from someone who's been there, done that and wants you to benefit from his mistakes and from the wisdom he has gained. The writer manages to address some serious concerns without taking himself too seriously and with a great deal of humor. His observations are often simple yet profound and insightful. He takes you into his confidence, sharing his personal experiences, in a very honest, real and vulnerable way. I walked away feeling as if I'd just had a long conversation with a close, trusted friend (or maybe a therapist!). I think so many people just go through the motions of parenting without giving it much thought, without really considering the best way to handle or approach various issues. Patrick Talley's book will inspire parents to give parenting issues the thought and attention they deserve." (Sondee from Houston)

"This is an important book!" (Michelle M. from Portland, OR)

"Excellent rules. Tears came to my eyes when I read the part about your daughter's insight into why she was biting her baby brother. Children have an incredible wisdom that we seem to forget or bury as adults. One of the greatest gifts I've been given are life lessons from my son. When I can find it in myself to listen to his wisdom, I grow and become a better parent. This glimpse into your book encourages me to read more and share it with others--mothers and fathers, divorced or not." (H.S. from the Mid-West)

"Patrick - stepping into his brilliance." (Suzanne T. from Spring Branch, TX)

"I think it's fantastic. Great info and anecdotes in a non judgmental writing style. I will definitely be forwarding the book to ALL of my single friends with kids." (Frank V. from Houston Texas)

"Patrick has learned wisdom far beyond his years... both from his experience as a divorced dad and from having become a perceptive student of mankind. Around 1970, I watched my own parents go through an especially painful divorce and over time have seen many poignant parallels between Patrick and my own Dad...The lessons Patrick shares via his experiences are certain to help thousands of dad's to make their way through this tough experience with far less anxiety than would otherwise be the case." (Jay D. from Houston)

"Patrick has always placed his children first. His relationship with his kids illustrates what we all could strive for." (Stacey F. from Texas)

"I'm diggin' your views and insights on parenting." (Hilary Goff Shirven from Peoria, IL)

"A book for parents raising kids anywhere on the planet." (David G. from London, U.K.)

"I think the book is great! I found it very easy to read and I found the book very interesting and entertaining. You had great stories and good advice." (Nini W. from Colombia S.A.)

Thank you for taking the time to read my little book. This book was a lifetime in the making – my lifetime! It started with the lessons I learned from my own big ol' goofy family. We literally put the FUNK in dysfunctional! In addition to those lessons, I have included lessons learned from parenting my two kiddos from diaper-babies to young adults. Over those years, I executed with elegance and stumbled as if I were wearing clown-shoes. This stumbling gave my children the "sand to make their pearls". The resulting Rules have been distilled over many years and through much of the noise level which was quite high during some of those parenting moments. With the noise now "stilled" and looking back in the rear-view mirror of parenting, these Rules can now be classified as WISDOM. These Rules will help you be the parent you want to be.

5319130R0

Made in the USA
Lexington, KY
27 April 2010